Lessons from a CEO's Journal

Leading Talent and Innovation

Kim E. Ruyle

Published by Inventive Talent Consulting, LLC
Coral Gables, Florida.

ISBN: 0692223754
ISBN 13: 9780692223758

Library of Congress Control Number: 2014910598
Inventive Talent Consulting, Coral Gables, FL

Talent innovates. Talent executes. Talent drives organizational performance.

www.inventivetalent.com

What Readers Think...

Lessons from a CEO's Journal

If you "don't know Jack" then you need to! This is a CEO who "gets it" and has the self-awareness and insight to share with us the wit and wisdom that comes with addressing business problems and finding solutions. We need more of "Leaders teaching Leaders," and this is a great example. Well worth the easy read.

> Richard M. Vosburgh, PhD—Vice-Chairman of the Board at HR People & Strategy (HRPS) and President at RMV Solutions LLC

We focus on employees and customers, and this book really hits the nail on the head regarding the importance of talent, innovation, and culture in the workplace.

> Keith S. Everson—President & CEO at Sussex IM

Kim Ruyle's *Lessons from a CEO's Journal: Leading Talent and Innovation* is insightful, imaginative and quite invaluable. Entertaining and easy to read, this "journal" details practical approaches to critical talent issues that can readily be applied in most organizations. I would highly recommend this book to anyone managing a business, a function or a workgroup who is looking to develop and drive a high performance culture.

> Chris Cimitile—Director, Organizational Development & Learning at Cricket Wireless (an AT&T Company)

Kim's book is a must-read for any leader who wants to successfully manage an enterprise or team by getting the most from its people. It is valuable for any professional whose job involves any aspect of talent management. As an HR professional involved in leadership development, this book really resonated with me, and I appreciate how Kim connects key talent concepts to day-to-day business dealings and challenges. Writing it as a journal makes the book non-technical and very easy reading. Entrepreneurs can especially relate to the style and content. I plan to provide the book to my company's leaders and to my HR team.

> George Boué, SPHR, CPC—Vice President of Human Resources at Stiles Corporation

As an author and talent management expert, Kim delivers what you need to know to leverage talent development and drive innovation. As both an art and science, Kim delivers his proven methodology and talent management expertise enabling readers to understand and influence critical talent development decisions. Each chapter delivers actionable, proven strategies as he shares decades of trend leading experience and proven techniques.

> John T. Mooney ACC, SPHR—Director of Organizational Development & Learning at Zodiac Aerospace

Kim's book is a really enjoyable way for leaders to sharpen their skills! Who doesn't want to absorb the wisdom of a successful CEO as he enjoys a leisurely-but-pensive Caribbean cruise?! You get advice for succeeding as a leader through the whole talent-management life cycle, and building leaders who can innovate and lead the future. It's a wonderful tale rooted in great science, and it will help leaders at any career stage be BETTER leaders."

> Cory Bouck—Author of T*he Lens of Leadership: Being the Leader Others WANT to Follow*

As a 20-year HR practitioner, I can say that the stories Jack shares are a rich, candid and "simple but sophisticated" source for refreshing our ideas on people management. I really liked the candid language and the extraordinary pragmatism of the stories. Thank you, Kim, for introducing us to Jack!

> Francesco Rossetti—General Manager of Human Resources Europe at Johnson Electric

This is an excellent read, a must for a seasoned HR practitioner. I couldn't put it down. I found myself chuckling as I have been caught in many of the traps myself.

> David Twitchell, PHR, CCP, CBP—Vice President of Human Resources at New Hampshire Catholic Charities

Kim's book on talent management nails it! The narrative point of view is a great way to capture the stream of consciousness about how a CEO thinks and feels about talent management.

Jacquelyn H. Wolf, PhD—SVP & Chief Human Resources Officer at LyondellBasell, Inc.

Very readable and engaging. I found myself getting pulled into Jack's world and making connections with my own. This book crystallizes a difficult, complex subject and makes it a conversation with a guy who has been there. It's a great tool for educating leaders who are involved in talent development.

Dennis Rohrs, SPHR—Director of Human Resources at Fort Wayne Metals

The countless people leaders and executives that Kim has taught and coached will recognize some the stories. Those who have not had the pleasure of working with Kim will be introduced to his straight-forward, common sense style. I heartily recommend this book for CEOs looking to move their organization in a different direction and for any aspiring CEO or manager who wants to improve their organization.

Charles (Chuck) Hughley – General Manager of Human Resources Americas at Johnson Electric

Author's Note

After more than 30 years working to understand and improve the performance of individuals, teams, and organizations, I've seen that success for many leaders hinges on their ability to: 1) effectively leverage talent, and 2) drive innovation and manage the change required to innovate. This book is for senior leaders who are concerned with these two capabilities.

I've written articles and other books on talent management that cite references to provide research and empirical evidence. There is empirical and research support for these contents, too, but I've elected to write a narrative, a story told in the voice of a retired CEO. The voice is conversational, and there are few embedded references. For those interested, I've appended a list of books recommended for further reading.

Jack, the narrator, is a fictional composite of several CEOs and other senior leaders that I've worked with over the past 30 years. Although he's fictional, I know Jack. Like so many other senior leaders, he's smart, stubborn, opinionated, and irreverent. Jack has grown businesses profitably and been financially rewarded for it. And just as most other leaders, he's had as many failures as he has successes. Over the course of a seven-day cruise, Jack reminisces on his career by journaling what he's learned about leveraging talent to drive innovation and business success.

Kim E. Ruyle

Coral Gables, Florida

Foreword

by Bob Eichinger

Coincidentally, my wife coerced me into taking the very same cruise as Jack. Like Jack, I was bored and on the hunt for something to do. Also like Jack, I'm a retired CEO. I had a series of talent management firms and consultancies and have written several books and created many tools for managers and organizations to use to better acquire, develop and deploy talent. I consider myself a talent management expert.

We were frequently seated in the dining room next to Jack's table, and I overheard (no, I was not intentionally eavesdropping!) many of his conversations. I quickly found out he was writing a journal on his life lessons about talent management and that he was discussing some of his thoughts with his companions at the dinner table.

At first, I was amused that an amateur was attempting to write about talent management. What could he possibly know? I have a PhD and 50 years of experience in the talent management business. How could he possibly know as much as I do? All he had done in his career is create and run companies! How could you learn about people by just running companies?

Curious, I began to sit next to him on the deck while he was writing his journal. I covered my surveillance by reading a book on the history of graphic arts.

Periodically he would leave his deckchair to take a swim or get a snack and he would leave his journal and his glasses behind. I began to take a peek. I read his notes on acquiring, onboarding, developing, and deploying people. I irritatingly found all of his ideas to be correct, meaning that they matched mine. Even more irritating was the fact that some of his ideas were new and innovative, beyond what I knew!

Over the course of the cruise, I was able to peek and read most of his jottings about talent management. They are for the most part correct and backed by the research. I also thought they were very practical, seeing that he learned them by trial and error rather than from a book.

I thought about introducing myself as a leader in the field of talent management, but he seemed to be doing fine without me.

As we were debarking, he did turn to me and ask whether I had enjoyed reading his journal! Surprised, I said yes I did. And I added a suggestion to publish it because I think others will enjoy it and gain from it. Jack smiled. I knew he knew!

Robert W. Eichinger, PhD
COO, Team Telligent, LLC
Vice Chairman (Retired), Korn Ferry International
Co-Founder and CEO (Retired), Lominger International

Contents

My Point of View

Day 1: December 30th, Florida Coast

Let's get a couple of things clear right off the bat. First, this is a work of fiction. If it turns out to be good fiction, like all good fiction, it will reveal something new, some previously undiscovered truths. Or, it will reveal familiar truths in fresh and surprising ways. For you, I hope it does both.

My journal entries are mostly autobiographical, but still fiction. We might as well face it, autobiographies are mostly a crock. All memories are more or less incomplete and inaccurately reconstructed. Mine are no exception.

Second thing to be clear about, I'm no writer. I'm Jack Smidt, an engineer turned businessman. And I figure the best way to get my thoughts down is to just write it like I'd say it. So be warned. If you continue reading you'll encounter a smattering of coarse language and political incorrectness.

As I write, I'm sitting on a small balcony on the ass-end (aft, for you nautical types) of a cruise ship watching the Ft. Lauderdale skyline fade in the distance. The balcony is just outside my port side 10th-level suite, relatively spacious accommodations on the ship, but much smaller than my workshop at home. Given a choice, I'd be there in my workshop now doing something productive—tuning my '66 GTO hotrod or building a custom stock for my Weatherby rifle. Instead, I'm here watching the Florida coast fade behind the wake and writing in an effort to feel productive.

Tomorrow is the last day of a momentous year. I turned 70 just a few weeks ago, coincidentally the same day I sold a minority equity stake in my latest business for 70 million bucks. Given this 70-70 coincidence, you might be thinking that I could have gotten more, that I settled for 70 million dollars for the symmetry, gave in to some sentimental impulse to accept 70k large on my 70th birthday.

You'd be wrong. I'm not a dimwit. Fact is, I used my looming birthday to negotiate a price premium—yes, a premium—by irrationally insisting that no way I'd take less than 70 million in this, my 70th year.

The buyer wanted my business, or at least a piece of it. Really wanted it. Had to have it. I knew that and figured he'd read my negotiating point as the silly whim of an old fart slipping into dementia. Who the hell sets a sale price based on a birthday? Rather than spin his wheels using logical argument and skillful negotiation on a supposed imbecile, he just bit the bullet and coughed up my asking price.

Don't believe for a minute that business deals are always rational, the result of detailed financial analysis. Financial analysis is often just the cover needed to justify the intuition (or irrational urge) of the buyer. Most acquisitions never turn out the way you anticipate, but more on business valuations, intangible value, and intuition later.

By referring to selling a piece of my "latest" business, I don't mean to imply that I've had a string of businesses that have netted me millions. Yes, I've been involved in several ventures over the years, but truth is, most of them flirted with failure. A couple did fail, and a couple of others were modestly successful.

I ran my last business for 20 years, and it was reasonably successful. But even in my swan song, I believe I made many mistakes. The business succeeded, to some extent, in spite of me, not because of me. For the foreseeable future, I'll chair the board, but as of today I've officially turned the day-to-day management over to others. I'm putting some distance now between me and the business. Just like the Florida Coast.

It was Betsy, my wife, who insisted I accompany her on this, my first, and I expect my last, cruise. I love her dearly and am trying to keep an open mind, but the idea of being a captive and forced to endure what other people consider to be relaxation and entertainment makes me want to jump overboard now before we're too far out at sea.

Betsy's idea is for me to finally relax for one full week, to ring in my first New Year as a retiree in the Caribbean, my just desserts for 70 years spent working my butt off. One day lounging in a deck chair for each decade of toil.

Should be easy, right? Not for me. I don't much appreciate tourists or their schlock. For me, the three least desirable vacation destinations are Las Vegas, Orlando, and Hell—and not necessarily in that order.

But now I find myself on a cruise ship, which appears to be the literal definition of a tourist trap. And even if I keep to myself and avoid the schlock, there's no way I'm going to be able sit around for seven days doing nothing. So I figured what the hell, why not use the opportunity to do something constructive? Why not reflect on my career and record some reflections in a journal?

This is it. My journal. Some might call my project "journaling" or think of it as an old fogey's version of blogging. For me, it's just writing, but it's significant because it clarifies my thoughts and commits them to posterity. And if you're reading this journal, count me as pleasantly surprised. Not surprised that I finished—I finish, by God, what I start. But pleasantly surprised that the journal of my seven-day Caribbean cruise found an audience.

Over the years, I think I've learned a few things about business, and finally, in this journal, I'm going to write down some of those lessons. I have no illusions. I'm fairly bright, but I'm not a full-fledged genius, and my writing will never rival the works of Drucker, Porter, Charan and other business gurus. Too bad. I love those guys and devour their books. But I'm realistic, so rather than attempting to write a business masterpiece, I will write a narrative to illustrate some key lessons I've learned from my businesses.

Now before you toss my journal in the dustbin, let me assure you that I won't tell you my life's story. I could regale you with stories about me, like the time I went to Alaska to fish for halibut and nearly drowned or the time I was arrested in a bar in Nogales or another time when I was chased by a bear in Wyoming. Those experiences are still exciting to me, but I've bored the hell out of my family and friends over the years with the retelling, and I'm not going to put you through that. However, you'll benefit from knowing a little about my background and a few high points of my career so you know the context for my point of view.

I grew up on a Minnesota farm, and there's no better place to grow up than on a farm. You learn to work. You learn about life and death and sex. You learn to solve problems, to be resourceful, be practical. You learn that there are a lot of shitty jobs to do (literally shitty, sometimes) but they all need to be done. And none of them are beneath you. Entitlements don't slop the hogs or bring in the crops.

One of the great tragedies created by the demise of the family farm is that we don't have farm kids entering the job market like we did 50 years ago. I never had a farm kid— boy or girl—that turned out to be a bad hire. Never. But more about this later.

Funny that I can reminisce now about growing up on the farm and appreciate what the experience did for me, but I didn't appreciate it so much when I was 18. I just wanted to get off the farm and see the world. So I joined the Army and in a bitter twist of irony got shipped to Oklahoma. I didn't get much geographical exposure in the Army, but I did get a very different view of the world. I shared a barracks with other 18-year-old kids from all over the country. Different ethnicities. Different eccentricities. Different values. So I learned quite a bit about the world in the Army.

And I also learned to weld. I was a hell of a welder. Loved it, worked hard to be the best. And if not the best, I was pretty close to it. At 21, I finished my tour of duty and returned to Minnesota, but not to the farm.

I went to Minneapolis and worked various union jobs— welding for the ironworkers and operating engineers, mostly. Nice thing about welding is it gives you time to dream. You drop the hood and watch the bright light and dream. When I wasn't dreaming about women, I dreamt about running my own business.

So being a man of action, I bought a 1-ton truck, lots of tools, and a portable welding rig. At 24 I was hiring myself out for all kinds of welding projects. That was my first business, and I did it all—fab, hard surfacing, and repair using stick, heli-arc, MIG, flux-core, and gas torches. I welded mild steel, alloy steel, stainless, cast iron, and aluminum. I did some light machining and took on unusual and challenging repair jobs.

A local contractor by the name of Donny frequently hired me to do contract jobs. He was a wheeler-dealer with a flair for invention. The guy was sometimes unhinged and unzipped, but it's often the crazies who change the world. Anyway, he had this idea to build a batch plant to produce light-weight concrete—light weight because it was full of air bubbles—concrete foam, so to speak.

Donny asked me to manage the maintenance of his new plant, and that seemed like a good opportunity to stretch myself and learn something new on the job but also have a predictable schedule that would allow me to go to school. I enrolled in a mechanical engineering program and managed plant maintenance nights and between classes during the day.

For four years I really didn't sleep, just studied and worked and occasionally napped. That's pretty much been my pattern for my whole life—I nap when I can no longer keep my eyes open. I suppose I'm violating all kinds of rules for brain and body health, but screw it. I hate to waste time sleeping, and my routine seems to work for me.

Five years in, Donny shut down his cellular concrete venture. His idea was good, but business success is largely a matter of timing, and I think he was ahead of his time. He lost a boatload of money in the venture, but he was philosophical about it, and that had a huge impact on me.

Up to that point I think I'd always subconsciously feared
failure, but I remember Donny saying that what made
our country great was that there were people who took
risks and worked their ass off to be successful. He said
bankruptcy was part of the equation, a special variable
that enabled us to be the greatest job creation engine the
world's ever seen. I guess I knew that in principle from the
farm. Farmers are hard-working risk-takers, and I'd seen
my share go bankrupt. But it was being part of this venture
when I was about 30 years old that made me begin to truly
appreciate the role of entrepreneurs.

Over the next 20 years, I started at least half a dozen
ventures and participated in several others. Most were fab
shops that manufactured products I designed—snowplows,
grain augers, and wood furnaces, for example. I partnered
once with a couple of other guys to design and manufacture
specialized lift truck attachments. I even started a
software company that created programs for maintenance
management.

None of these ventures netted me much financial gain. For
the most part, my businesses supported me and my family
and enabled me to pay my bills, sometimes in fits and
starts. The only thing really certain was the stress. It kept
me on my toes. Never bored. Always wondering, would
I get that next project? Would I make payroll? Would I
survive? Would I keep my sanity?

My public school education was solid, but it seems that in
some ways I really didn't start learning until I entered the
Army. And when I started my first business, my education
kicked into high gear. Sure, I had confidence in spades,
but I knew squat, almost nothing about business or about
myself. Boy, did I get schooled.

I lacked self-awareness

Because I lacked self-awareness, I didn't understand my strengths and weaknesses, especially my weaknesses. I created problems by over-developing a few of my strong points. For example, over-using my above-average intelligence turned me into an arrogant smart-ass. I don't need to tell you that an arrogant smart-ass tends to alienate customers, employees, and the public at large.

My lack of self-awareness led me to ignore my weaknesses. And they are many. Too many to enumerate, but I can summarize like this: if we're talking about anything that's not categorized as technical or inanimate, we're probably talking about one of my weaknesses.

Raters on my first 360 assessment gave me some pretty direct feedback in the comments section, including these three:

1. "Jack's always in a hurry and seems impatient when interrupted. It's hard to know when and how to approach him."

2. "I've seen Jack roll his eyes and sigh heavily in meetings when he doesn't like what someone is saying. People are afraid to disagree with him."

3. "Give us a chance to figure things out. I feel like I'm never working fast enough to make you happy, and it sucks when you step in and finish something for me."

Feedback like that and my frequent failures in developing relationships, negotiating, and leading change made me desperate enough to turn inward and begin learning about myself. I began to listen to feedback from others. I began to ask for it.

Frequent reflection has become a habit. No, I don't sit cross-legged while chanting and fondling crystals. I don't get carried away by the chiming of Tibetan singing bowls. Harmonic overtones don't send me to a spiritual place. If you're into that sort of thing, knock yourself out. Me, I'm about as far away from a New Age navel-gazer as you can get. I've generally got tobacco in my cheek and cowboy boots on my feet, for God's sake. But I do think. I do reflect. I reflect after a meeting. After a difficult conversation. After winning a deal. After losing a deal. I make it a practice to pause to consider how things went down, what I did effectively, and not so effectively.

I've walked many miles down the road to self-awareness, but my journey won't end until I stop breathing. And when I relate to you my motives and values, feel free to be skeptical. You should be. I'm still surely self-deceived in some ways and engage in unconscious self-promotion. So it goes with all of us. None of us fully understands his own motives and values, and it's impossible to ever truly understand those of another person.

With that forewarning, here's my self-assessment of my personal motives and values: I am driven by a need for achievement, and I measure achievement by my reputation first and by the money I make as a secondary scorecard. I like to win and hate to lose. I like to be viewed as an expert. I take pride in my work ethic and my ability to solve tough problems.

I'm not particularly altruistic, but I do try to help people and occasionally give to charity. My preference, though, is to help others by giving opportunities for rewarding employment. And I'm not just referring to financial rewards. The jobs I've had have provided me with skills, purpose, and a sense of accomplishment.

Any honest employment teaches values and self-respect. A good job goes further and, in addition to providing for financial needs, engages the intellect and meets psychological needs. What could be more valuable? And in that regard, I've done quite a lot for others. Add up all the people I've employed over five decades, and it numbers in the thousands. Think what you will, but I figure the social value of all the taxes I've given over the years to our thriftless government bureaucracy doesn't begin to compare to the social value provided by the employment opportunities I've created.

Julie is a good example. A twenty-something-year-old single mother with a high school education, she came to us as a temp employee in production. We taught her to drive lift trucks, and she worked for a while on our loading dock. When we needed a production scheduler, we took her on as a full-time employee. From there she moved into purchasing, got an accounting degree, moved to accounts payable, became an accounting manager, and now is controller. I attended her daughter's college graduation. At the reception, Julie talked to me about her career and what it has meant to her and her daughter. All the while, her eyes sparkled.

Julie and so many other employees like her have helped me learn about myself. To a large extent, they've defined my contribution to the world and help me feel like I've had a small part in making the world a better place. Not that I'm into self-congratulation. I've never felt self-satisfied. Quite the contrary, in fact.

I lacked business acumen

By the time I was 40 years old, I was feeling frustrated, very impatient with my perceived lack of accomplishment. I had run several marginally successful businesses that were built on my own particular skill set. I could bend, cut, machine, and weld metal. And I could design mechanical devices. Nothing wrong with those skills, but they're not unique and not enough to create the kind of business I wanted to build.

By all accounts I guess I should have been satisfied, but I wasn't. Far from it. It's difficult to explain how badly I wanted to achieve more. I needed to make a mark on the world. Running a small regional business that manufactured grain augers or furnaces wasn't enough. Hitting singles wasn't enough. I desperately wanted to knock one out of the park, but the home run was ever elusive.

My frustration led me to enroll in an executive MBA program at Kellogg in Chicago. One of the courses was on strategy. The case studies were interesting and led to thought-provoking discussions in class about strategy differentiation. I remember feeling like those discussions were high-wattage floodlights, raising painful blisters on my shortcomings.

It wasn't that I hadn't tried to be strategic. I'd certainly considered how to differentiate my products and segment my customers. I'd given thought to my value proposition, my business model, and my value chain. But up until then, all my thinking had been relatively superficial. My MBA program caused me to dig deeply and reconsider everything I thought I knew about business strategy.

Some will probably disagree with me, but I think all the different models and viewpoints on strategy are simply different lenses to bring clarity to the differentiation of your business. You can examine your business through the lens of value proposition or the lens of business model or the lens of value chain. You might look through several lenses before you find the one that brings everything into focus for you. That's how it was for me.

When I looked through the lens of organizational capabilities, everything came into focus. It seems so simple now, but it was a profound lesson for me at the time. I realized that it's not enough to be the best at one or two things. Being highly skilled at welding and bending metal wasn't unique after all. Those skills alone didn't give me a competitive advantage. They didn't differentiate. They weren't a strategy. But I might be able to grow a dynamic business with a dominant competitive position by focusing on a unique combination of capabilities that were exceptionally deep and nearly impossible to replicate. I began thinking about how to identify those capabilities and accelerate their development to a level that would enable me to hit the home run.

Those capabilities started to be revealed within a year of completing my MBA when I was approached by a new customer who asked if my fab shop had the capabilities to design and build a specialized piece of equipment, an autoclave for processing complex composite parts. The customer was a supplier to the defense industry in the emerging composite materials industry.

This particular opportunity presaged lots of potential business, but what really captured my attention was the opportunity it represented to begin building that unique combination of capabilities I was seeking for competitive advantage.

As I write this, I'll admit to now feeling sheepish thinking about the assurances I provided to the customer. "Of course, we can meet your specs and budget. Chamber dimensions are no problem. Instrumentation? Sure, we can handle that."

Now I can see that I was certainly exaggerating if not outright prevaricating, but that wasn't my mindset or intention at the time. Even though we had never designed or built anything resembling an autoclave, let alone something with the controls and instrumentation this project required, I never doubted our ability to do it.

After closing the deal, I assembled my team and excitedly described the project. They weren't nearly as excited as I was. Sideways looks, skepticism, maybe even a little panic in their eyes. But I encouraged them to rise to the challenge. "We are first and foremost problem solvers! We are the right team for this job!" I believed it and needed them to believe it. Accepting the challenge to design and build our first autoclave was a turning point.

We made a decent profit, but much more importantly, we learned a lot. We were stretched. We followed that project by building other specialized production tools that incorporated sophisticated controls and instrumentation to handle and process advanced composite materials. The machines we designed and built had to handle high heat and pressure. We also designed and built tooling for composite manufacturing.

After that, every project we took on seemed to stretch us. We experimented. We discovered many methods that didn't work and a few that did. After nearly ten years and many custom projects for a handful of clients in the industry, we'd accumulated the unique set of competencies that no one else could match. It was time to take a leap and create a new venture.

The new business, the one in which I recently sold equity, is a manufacturer of composite parts, primarily for the aerospace and automotive industries. The business is vertically integrated to the extent we design and build almost all of our production equipment and the tooling required for parts manufacture. We have achieved a dominant competitive position.

I didn't understand talent management

A lot of what I've learned has been the result of my mistakes. I've sometimes hired the wrong people. I've attempted to engage them inappropriately. I've done a poor job of delegating and developing. One of my biggest mistakes was thinking that other people are like me. They're not, thank God.

Along the way, I had help from Isabel, whom I'd initially hired to be a production coordinator. She was incredibly bright and motivated and energetic. After watching her succeed in a variety of progressively challenging positions, I asked her to take on responsibility for human resources and join my management team.

Isabel's growth kept up with the growth of my business. For 20 years she was my coach and confidante. She was also my provocateur in the positive sense of the word. She challenged me to develop a more rigorous point of view about talent, and I challenged her too.

Our collaboration resulted in the development of a very robust and unique set of organizational capabilities developed by leveraging our talent. Much of what I will write about in the following pages will illustrate how we leveraged our talent to achieve success.

When asked, every executive will tell you how important their people are, how their enterprise rises or falls on the quality of their talent. And for some organizations, this is more than lip service. Some organizations are indeed masters at leveraging talent. They are highly disciplined, almost scientific in their approach to talent management. They rigorously attract, develop, engage, and deploy talent, and it's not because they have highly capable HR professionals (which they surely do). It's because they have the most skilled line managers. In fact, the operational managers in these organizations are often more skilled at talent management than the HR professionals in lesser organizations.

Early in my career, talent management wasn't a top priority for me. By the end of my career, it was my number one priority. My business strategy might have been world class, but I needed talent to execute it. My business processes may have been perfectly engineered to deliver top-quality products and services without friction, but only talent could design, manage, and continuously improve those processes. My people managed our financial capital and the supply chain. My people were the drivers of customer loyalty. My people were innovators, and innovation was the engine of our profitable growth. And my people gave texture to our organizational culture, something nearly impossible for the competition to copy. What follows is the approach we used to get the most from our talent.

Recruiting Talent

Day 2: December 31st, Caribbean Sea

It's the second day of my cruise, and a beautiful day has dawned here in the Caribbean. The weather is perfect, and the seas are calm. This part of the world with its beaches, palm trees, and laid-back lifestyle is widely viewed as paradise, but I have no plans to move South for my retirement. I guess I don't want to get too comfortable. Does that sound twisted? Maybe I've got some kind of perverse sense of pride in the severe weather we have in the Midwest. Sure, I know there are occasional hurricanes in the Caribbean, and they're horrific. But on the whole, the Caribbean climate is tranquil.

In the Midwest, we have the brutally cold, interminable winters. The abrupt summers with withering heat and humidity. It seems we're never more than a few days away from some major weather event. Violent thunderstorms are commonplace. So are white-out blizzard conditions. We occasionally endure hailstorms that pummel us with golf ball-sized chunks of ice and tornados that devastate everything in their path. The weather is crappy so often that we really do appreciate it when it's a nice day. Personally, I like the variety.

People are like the Midwest weather. There's amazing variety. Sometimes they disappoint us, and sometimes they delight us. And just as the meteorologist works to predict the weather, a very important part of our jobs as leaders is to make predictions about people.

Every time we hire someone, we're making a prediction, placing a bet. When we select someone for a critical assignment or promotion, we're drawing inferences and making a prediction. And when we decide to invest time, energy, and resources in developing an employee, we're gambling that the investment will provide a good return. Predicting how people will perform in given situations is one of the most critical skills for leaders.

Making predictions about people

When it comes to understanding and sizing up people, most of us suck. We don't think we suck. We trust our intuition. We believe our gut accurately tells us when a candidate's got the right stuff. This is probably the most common blind spot for leaders. Leaders think they're good at reading and selecting people, but most are wrong just as often as they are right.

In some respects, the way our brain has evolved works against us. In order for our species to survive, we've developed sensory systems and brains that continuously and quickly size up our environment to identify threats and opportunities. Other people are part of our environment, and for survival reasons our brains make instant discriminations when we encounter someone unfamiliar. Discrimination isn't always bad. In fact, it's a biological necessity.

When you meet me for the first time, your brain will make many assessments in a matter of seconds, and for the most part, you'll be largely unaware of the discriminating view your brain is creating. Regarding employment potential, especially leadership potential, you'll view me more positively if I'm tall. I'm not.

You'll be drawn to me if I fit your cultural stereotype of what makes a person attractive—facial symmetry and proportional size and spacing of features (Betsy thinks I'm adorable). As soon as I open my mouth and start speaking, you will be assessing my intelligence. You'll infer that I'm a more confident and capable leader if my posture is erect, my handshake firm and dry, and my voice steady and deep. You'll almost assuredly feel some level of revulsion if I'm ugly or fat.

To the degree you have familiarity with any human characteristic, you also have a degree of related bias. You, yes you, have some degree of gender bias, racial bias, and age bias. Don't tell me you don't. You might as well tell me you never break the speed limit, your kids are all perfectly darling geniuses, and your dog smells good. We are all biased, and no one is conscious of all their biases.

Personally, I don't think it's possible to totally overcome these tendencies. Remember, the discrimination process is hard-wired in our brains and a requirement for survival. I do think it's possible for us to better understand our biases and mitigate their effects. We probably don't need to obsess about this, but we'd all do well to develop a greater awareness of our biases. If you want references on this, just do a web search for neuroscience and bias or, alternatively, for neuroleadership.

In addition to the unconscious biases that are of a general nature and shared by most other people, we have biases that are personal and related to our own values and background. Think about the people you call friends, the people you truly like on a personal level. It's a good bet that they're like you in many ways. They probably share similar interests. They care about the things you care about. They like what you like and disdain what you disdain. They're likely to come from a similar socioeconomic background. It's natural. It's hard for me to imagine meeting a welder from the Midwest who grew up on a farm that I wouldn't like. We naturally choose people we like to be our friends and to hire as employees.

There's certainly nothing wrong with liking the people with whom we work. That's a good thing. But we need to understand how our biases and lack of sophistication about how to rigorously assess people lead us to make errors in discrimination.

Since the term discrimination has so many negative connotations, I'll reluctantly succumb to political correctness and from this point forward use the term differentiation. The ability to rigorously and accurately differentiate talent is one of the most important skills we can learn as leaders.

The most effective organizations are masters at differentiating talent. They make more accurate predictions about how people will perform in a given situation. They have a well-articulated employee value proposition that differentiates their organization from other potential employers. And they use rigorous, robust, and cost-effective methods for talent selection.

Importance of the employee value proposition

Before we explore the differentiation required for selecting new hires, let's consider how differentiation applies to attracting talent to our organization. Why do your customers buy from you rather than from your competition? The answer to that question is your unique value proposition. Why do potential employees choose to work for you even when they have other opportunities? The answer to that question is your employee value proposition.

It's commonly understood that strategic effectiveness involves clearly spelling out how the firm is being positioned in the competitive landscape, the customers it serves, and the value it provides to those customers. An effective strategy and value proposition will also clarify those customers that are not served, those who are strategically and intentionally excluded. An effective employee value proposition works the same way. It attracts some candidates (the right ones) and repels others. Here's an example of what I believe is an effective employee value proposition:

> *We design and manufacture advanced composite components that are used in state-of-the art aircraft, automobiles, and specialized machinery. We're not just passionate about what we do, we're fanatical. We are technical experts and love to solve complex problems. We are invigorated by technical challenges that frighten others. We love to innovate. We are a meritocracy. We don't tolerate bureaucracy, mediocrity, or excuses. We reward technical excellence, initiative, and ingenuity.*

Do you have a pretty good sense about what this organization values? Do you think you have some insight into the culture? An idea of what it would be like to work there? Who would be successful? Who would not be successful?

A good employee value proposition provides insight into not only who's likely to be successful, but also who's likely to fail. When we have a choice between two opportunities, jobs included, most of us choose the one in which we're least likely to fail. I like the statement above because it accurately reflects the values of senior leadership and is aligned with the desired culture of the organization. It should appeal to the kind of prospective employees who will readily fit in the organization. It should be distasteful to prospective employees who won't fit in the organization.

Now, compare the above employee value proposition to this one:

> *Our people are our most important asset. We provide rewarding career opportunities and strive to be the employer of choice in our industry.*

Clearly, the second statement is about as good as no value proposition at all. In fact, I'd go so far as to say it would be better to not have any explicit value proposition than one that tries to be all things to all potential employees. If a good strategic value proposition for your firm intentionally excludes some potential customers, shouldn't your employee value proposition exclude some potential employees?

Give serious thought to how your employee value proposition can raise the bar and create a tighter, more focused, and easier-to-manage net for prospective talent. If you do so, you will be more efficient in recruiting, and your recruiting processes will yield higher-quality candidates.

Employees hired from a targeted pool of prospects will be more quickly productive and integrated into your culture. Give serious thought to preparing every hiring manager— better yet, every employee—to be able to effortlessly relate the employee value proposition to prospective employees.

Employee interviewing and selection

A differentiating employee value proposition will enhance your recruiting process by yielding a prospect pool that is of higher quality and more uniform. But you still need to differentiate prospects once you get them in the door to be interviewed. Differentiation in the selection process for new hires is absolutely essential.

I've certainly made my share of mistakes in this regard, especially early in my career when I hired people who were over-qualified and was then unable to keep them engaged. I've screwed up by hiring people who were highly skilled in some competencies but lacked other competencies that were critical to their success. I've paid dearly for these mistakes in severance costs, but more importantly, in the opportunity cost for the time and confusion involved in replacing the bad hire. There's also the incalculable cost of damage to employee morale and loss of my credibility because of the poor judgment I exercised as hiring manager. There should be absolutely no doubt about the importance of hiring right.

As an example of my bias getting in the way, I once hired a retired Army officer, a graduate of West Point, to be a general manager and oversee our manufacturing. Jeff had sterling credentials, but that didn't prevent almost immediate problems in production that were the result of his leadership style. While I was trying to promote initiative, reasonable risk-taking, and accountability, Jeff was accustomed to giving and following orders. He wasn't comfortable outside of a rigid chain of command and failed to adapt to our culture.

I remember the day I had half a dozen production workers crowd into my office to warn me of an impending mutiny on the production floor. The ringleader said, "Jeff says 'shit' and expects us all to squat. We're not a bunch of rookies out there. Would it hurt him to say please or ask nicely once in a while?" I dealt with the situation, but the turmoil created in my operations by that hiring mistake was very costly.

There are two important points to make related to this situation. First, Jeff was highly unusual in that, in spite of his experience as a military officer, he lacked flexibility and adaptability. In my experience, this is very rare. Theaters of modern warfare are defined by ambiguity and require soldiers who can adapt and learn on the fly. The modern military still maintains a chain of command, of course, but its leadership development programs are first-rate and among the best training grounds in the world to learn flexibility and adaptability. I'm not serving up this first point in defense of my bad hiring decision, but rather to go on record as a strong believer in the value of the military as a source of great employees.

The second point and primary lesson I took away from the experience is that I let Jeff's excellent credentials and my bias for military experience blind me to the full picture. Prominent characteristics, good or bad, can blind us to the full picture. This is often where our biases derail the selection process. It seems that every time I've made a hiring mistake, it's because I fell victim to my biases and became so fixated on one or two attributes related to the hiring criteria that I lost sight of the big picture.

The hiring picture, in my view, includes seven fundamental elements that should be considered to adequately differentiate and select any new employee. This should be basic knowledge for all hiring managers, not just for HR staff. However, from what I've seen, most managers focus on two or three elements, overlook the rest, and are overly influenced by their biases. The result is that managers will hire a candidate they like (i.e., that is similar to them) as long as they meet a couple of the selection criteria. Making good hiring decisions is so important, it's worthwhile to review seven selection criteria that differentiate candidates.

Seven dimensions of selection

1. *Motivation.* Let's deal with this one first because it's a well-known price-of-admission attribute and is relatively easy to assess. What we're referring to here is a combination of energy and desire for achievement. If you've articulated your employee value proposition and clearly spelled out what it takes to be successful in your firm, finding motivated candidates should not be difficult.

   Virtually everyone starts a new job being highly motivated. People want to succeed. Unless your candidate is desperate for a job and only applying for something to tide them over until their dream job opens up, they will likely be motivated to impress you and advance.

   Normally, you don't have to specifically interview for this characteristic. Check the resume or work history to look for evidence of persistence, resilience, and ambition. You'll notice that I don't include education in my

Motivation

Intelligence

Personality

Experience

Technical Competencies

Leadership Competencies

Values and Cultural Fit

list of essentials because it's not a universal requirement, although I do recognize education serves as table stakes for certain roles. Additionally, education might tell you more about motivation than it does about any of the elements that follow, even intelligence.

Personally, I wouldn't spend time interviewing someone if I had any doubts about their motivation. If you're in an interview situation and aren't sure, ask them to describe the most ambitious goals they've achieved and how they overcame obstacles to reaching their goals.

2. *Intelligence.* Given a choice between two otherwise equivalent candidates, you'd hire the smarter one, right? Intelligence accounts for a lot of the variance between successful and less successful employees. We're intuitively attracted to people who are quick, intellectually curious, and like to solve problems.

Intelligence deserves a spot on the list because I believe it's rarely explicitly addressed in the hiring process. I am not suggesting that you administer intelligence tests to candidates. I am suggesting that you make sure your recruiting people do pay attention to indicators of intelligence as they pre-screen candidates. Make sure your hiring managers are looking for signals during interviews so they can differentiate candidates on this dimension.

3. *Personality.* You don't necessarily want complete homogeneity of personalities in the workforce, but you do want harmony.

Personality impacts the way we get our work done, how we approach problems, interact with coworkers, and deal with stress and conflict. Look for personality characteristics that won't fit the team dynamics and organizational culture. When personality characteristics fall outside the norms of behavior in your workplace, you'll hear people described with terms such as arrogant, kiss-ass, nervous, suspicious, Machiavellian, pissy, confrontational, emotional, and passive-aggressive.

Some of the traits that most often influence job fit include self-confidence, sociability, and conscientiousness. Ignore personality at your own peril.

4. *Experience.* We learn what we need for success primarily through experience, by doing a job, but not all experience is created equal. It can be said that a candidate with ten years of experience who's not had variety and challenge has really just had one year of experience repeated ten times. Contrast that with a candidate who, over the course of ten years, has had three or four jobs that have been challenging and provided opportunity to learn different competencies. Obviously the edge goes to the second candidate. Evaluate experience for the variety and amount of stretch and challenge required of the candidate.

5. *Technical competencies.* Competencies are skills that can be measured and learned and contribute to success on the job. Technical

competencies are those specifically related to the job function or related area of expertise, and I believe they are almost always viewed as the top priority by hiring managers. It makes sense. After all, competence is the very definition of being able to do the job. We tend to hire people first and foremost for technical competence. Welders need to be able to weld. Accountants need to know how to count. And programmers need to be able to program.

Even though we hire people primarily for their technical competence, we almost never fire them for technical incompetence. Technical incompetence is relatively rare. It's the leadership competencies, or lack thereof, that get people into trouble. We fire people, in general, because the way they do their job is unacceptable. They're unreliable. They don't get along. They violate explicit policies or implicit cultural norms. I believe we place too much focus on differentiating candidates by way of technical competencies. I'm not saying you should ignore them. I'm saying that it probably makes sense to place more focus on key leadership competencies when selecting employees.

6. *Leadership competencies.* Skills such as conflict management, planning, negotiating, and listening are generalizable to all positions, and I'm referring to all such generalizable skills as leadership competencies. Put some thought into the nature of the job and the context in which it's performed so you can identify a handful of mission-critical leadership

competencies to differentiate candidates. If success in a job requires a reasonably high degree of skill in a particular competency, that competency can be considered mission-critical.

Usually there are more mission-critical competencies required than you can adequately assess through interviewing. Fortunately, some of these important competencies will probably be in high supply in the workforce and can be considered price-of-admission competencies. Most potential employees will have skills to focus on customers and achieve results, for instance. It's not so likely that many potential employees will be highly skilled in developing strategy, managing innovation, or motivating subordinates. Take the time to identify the mission-critical leadership competencies and use them to differentiate candidates.

7. *Values and cultural fit.* The first element we considered is motivation, a combination of energy and desire to succeed. We need to also consider the values that explain a person's motivation, the values that drive a person's behavior. Let's say you and your organizational culture place a very high value on commercial profit, experimentation, and outspoken challenge. A new employee who values philanthropy, certainty, and civility over your values will almost certainly be rejected just like the body rejects an unsuitable organ. Especially if you have a strong organizational culture—if you have little variation in what's deemed acceptable behavior—you're advised to differentiate for cultural fit.

Seven dimensions - one big picture

Remember my preference for farm kids? Throughout my career I actively recruited farm kids because I believed that, given my business needs, the pool of farm kids would have a higher percentage of good hires than most other pools. It was a way to reduce the uncertainty in making the hiring decision. That didn't mean I wouldn't encounter bad fits for my organization in the pool of prospective farm kids, but I took steps to even further improve my odds.

Because I recognized that I had a strong bias for farm kids, I took extra precautions to ensure I considered the big picture and differentiated on the seven dimensions above. Now, years later, I can say I never hired someone who grew up on a farm that didn't turn out to be a good employee.

No matter how much time you spend checking references and interviewing to assess candidates, you will never eliminate all uncertainty from your hiring decision. You have a responsibility to do as much as is reasonable to reduce uncertainty and adequately differentiate prospective employees.

Taken together, the above dimensions comprise a large part of the hiring picture. Each is required of all employees, and if you differentiate prospective employees on these dimensions and aren't derailed by your biases, you will make few hiring mistakes.

Approach to interviewing

Your interviewing methods can help or hinder your ability to differentiate prospective employees, but you're already an expert interviewer, right? Maybe. Maybe not. I sure thought I was a great interviewer, but on reflection, I'd say I was mediocre early in my career and got worse over time until I finally woke up later in my career. As I gained experience and took on greater responsibilities, I placed too much confidence in my intuition. I didn't prioritize my time in order to prepare. I didn't follow a consistent script and lost focus during the interview. My slide in interviewing effectiveness is typical.

In general, there's an inverse relationship between good interviewing techniques and position level. Junior hiring managers are more likely to prepare, follow a script, and take the interview seriously. Senior executives usually do a mediocre job at best. Most tend to be unprepared, get easily distracted, and don't focus on assessing the right dimensions. They change their approach from one candidate to another so their evaluation is inconsistent. As often as not, their interview turns into a BS session with the candidate.

To ensure our people used good interviewing techniques, we implemented an internal certification program for all interviewers that addressed a number of effective practices.

- ≈ Interviewers consistently assessed mission-critical competencies that were identified through job analysis and included in the job description. Every candidate, regardless of the position applied for, went through at least three interviews and was evaluated by at least six certified interviewers. There was at least one interview that focused on leadership competencies and another to focus on cultural fit.

- ≈ We used a structured, behavioral-based approach to interviewing that assured consistency and yielded a much more accurate assessment of the key dimensions. The idea is to follow a script that asks candidates to speak to actual experience rather than responding in hypotheticals. For example, you might ask, "What's your approach to resolving conflict between team members?" The problem with that approach is that it leaves the door open for the candidate to say anything that might be deemed a good response. Better to say, "Tell me about a time you resolved a difficult conflict between team members." This difference is significant. Interviewers were taught to listen for the candidate's thought process, specific actions taken, the results of the action, and what was learned.

≈ Interviewers were taught and given opportunity to practice interviewing skills. They learned to make time to prepare for the interview, to eliminate distractions so they could focus during the interview, and to keep the big picture in mind. They learned to take good notes to document what they learned in interviews. They practiced listening and posing follow-up questions so the interview was consistent from one candidate to another. Interviewers learned to spot patterns and themes related to all seven of our universal dimensions for differentiation. We also helped interviewers to understand and deal with their biases.

≈ After potential interviewers had demonstrated proficiency, we certified them and tried to pair them with a more experienced interviewer at first. In any case, all interviews were conducted in pairs, and this included interviews that I conducted as CEO. There was a uniform script used for each position, and, although both interviewers independently evaluated candidates and took extensive interview notes, they followed a script that ensured that only one person was asking questions related to any particular dimension during the interview.

≈ Hiring decisions were made by consensus of the six interviewers. Prior to any discussion, all interviewers submitted their interview notes and recommendation. They could vote to extend an offer to the candidate, pass on the candidate, or abstain because of reservations. Only after all the documentation was submitted did interviewers convene and talk through their insights and recommendations. If there were two or more votes to pass on the candidate, the conversation was generally short, but reservations were addressed in the discussions. In the end, we hired people that were fully supported by everyone or, worst case, in which no more than two of six people lacked enthusiasm but were at least cautiously supportive.

Without being dogmatic about it, I can say that our approach worked well for us and wasn't overkill. Hiring is far too important to take lightly or do in a sloppy manner. In spite of all we did, I found that I needed to constantly recognize and reinforce good hiring decisions and practices. My managers looked to me to be the example. It took effort to become an exemplary interviewer. If I hadn't personally made this a priority, I don't believe our efforts would have been sustainable.

Selection criteria for talent pools

One of the hardest things for me to figure out in the recruiting process was how high to set the bar for qualifications. We definitely want great talent, but how should we view a stellar candidate who's overqualified? Will we be able to keep an overqualified candidate engaged over the long term? Are we better off hiring people who will be stretched and value the development? Is it more important to hire for demonstrated competence or for potential?

These are not easy questions to answer. After wrestling with these issues, we developed slightly different guidelines for four candidate sub-populations, four differentiated talent pools. There's a lot to say about how to differentiate talent pools, but I'll save detailed information for a later discussion. For now, here's a brief description of these groups:

- *High potential generalists.* These were candidates who were selected for senior general management positions or at least expected to advance more quickly and further than the vast majority of other employees and to eventually serve in senior general management positions.

- *High potential specialists.* These were candidates who had extensive experience, deep expertise, and passion for a technical discipline. They were selected to be technical leaders or at least expected to advance rather quickly and to eventually serve in a senior position, perhaps leading a technical function.

- *People managers.* We differentiated those who were recruited for supervisor or mid-management positions yet not expected, at least initially, to advance to senior management.

≋ *Core employees.* These were the majority of
employees who certainly had potential to learn
and grow and advance in their career but were not
initially hired with the expectation that they would
rise to a senior management position. There was
always the possibility, though, that they could. And
some did.

Our strategy was to develop and promote from within
whenever possible, and nine out of ten times we were
interviewing for core employees. Every company needs a
build-versus-buy strategy for talent, and our preference
was for building talent. It's probably neither advisable nor
possible to only use one approach. Though we did our
best to aggressively groom talent and promote from within,
we occasionally had to recruit from outside for senior
positions, especially for high potential specialists.

We gave lots of consideration to how the seven fundamental
selection criteria are related to each of these talent pools.
Here's the viewpoint we developed:

≋ *Motivation.* A high degree of motivation was
a non-negotiable price-of-admission for every
prospective employee. In fact, candidates never
made it to an interview unless we saw solid evidence
of persistence, resilience, and ambition during the
pre-hire screening. This applied to all employees, all
talent pools, but we considered this dimension even
more closely for our high potentials. We considered
educational attainment to be an indication of
motivation as much as, even more so, than an
indication of intelligence.

≋ *Intelligence.* We placed a premium on intelligence
for all talent pools, but it was even more important,

considered absolutely essential, for high potential specialists. We wanted smart people across the board, but in our technical functions we aimed for brilliance. We didn't administer intelligence tests, but we explicitly looked for indications of intelligence when we pre-screened candidates and observed and listened carefully during interviews to validate those indications.

Pre screening provides an opportunity to look for work and academic accomplishments that reflect problem-solving abilities and general intelligence. Interviewing provides an opportunity to assess how the candidate uses vocabulary, responds to questions, and coherently articulates positions. Taken together, this information paints a pretty clear picture of intellectual horsepower.

Placing a premium on intelligence might backfire if you don't have the right type of business and organizational culture. Highly intelligent people are likely to get bored and become disengaged if they're not in an intellectually stimulating environment. It turned out that for us, our decision to prioritize intelligence for all talent pools was a primary enabler of our strategy to build talent and promote from within. This is probably the least malleable of all the dimensions, even less moldable than personality and values/cultural fit. Stupidity might not be forever— people can learn to wise up. But you don't want to be stuck with people who are far out of their depth.

≋ *Personality.* We put thought into what comprised a desirable general personality profile and how the profile would vary for the talent pools. In all candidates we wanted to see evidence of curiosity, collaboration, and adventure-seeking because our culture promoted experimentation, teamwork, and prudent risk taking. Red flags went up when we saw indications that candidates were sensitive to criticism, arrogant, or cautious. Since technical experts are stereotypically reserved and lack social skills, we probed for evidence of interpersonal and collaborative skills. We looked for evidence of a balance of empathy and directness in our people managers.

≈ *Experience.* We did the typical pre-screening of experience for all candidates and generally placed more value on variety and the degree of difficulty or challenge in experiences than similarity to the target position. The exception to this was for our high potential specialists who were valued for their deep expertise, which can only come from focused practice and experience.

Most of our evaluation of experience occurred prior to interviews. The last thing we wanted to do with valuable interview time was to waste it rehashing a resume. Our questions about experience during interviews was primarily to gain insight into the challenges candidates had faced, what they learned from those challenges, and how they applied what they learned.

≈ *Technical competencies.* We pre-screened for technical competencies and used little or no interview time on this dimension except for our high potential specialists. As a final step prior to extending an offer to one of these candidates, we asked them to present a 45-minute seminar for other technical employees. They were asked to present on an advanced technical topic for 30 minutes and then field questions for 15 minutes. This validated their technical savvy but also gave us valuable insight into their ability to communicate complex technical subjects and interact effectively with our other experts.

≈ *Leadership competencies.* We devoted at least one interview to assessing leadership competencies, and these interviews varied in content according to the talent pool. In every case, we used a structured, behavioral-based approach to address at least five competencies that were mission-critical and likely to be rare in the talent pool. For high potential generalists, we assessed competencies related to strategic thinking, motivating, a tolerance for ambiguity, conflict management, and others depending on the specific role. High potential specialists were assessed for conflict management, peer relationships, and ability to develop others. People managers were assessed for interpersonal skills, motivating, managerial courage, and ability to delegate and develop others effectively.

≈ *Cultural fit.* The assessment of values and cultural fit was perhaps the most important consideration, and we spent one interview focused on this dimension. I'm proud of the capability we developed to make good hiring decisions, but as indicated earlier, you can never remove all uncertainty from people decisions, and you'll always find that people sometimes delight you and other times disappoint you. When we made the occasional bad hire, more often than not the reason things didn't work out was that there was a lack of cultural fit.

We made this dimension a focus for every talent pool and did our best to ensure that candidates had motives and values that would fit with our organizational culture. A sense of entitlement was one of the factors we tried very hard to uncover in the values interview. We attracted highly skilled and accomplished people for our high potential positions. Sometimes those with a successful track record and assortment of credentials have a sense of entitlement that didn't fit our culture, which promoted a meritocracy.

Importance of learning agility

Learning agility is an important dimension that I didn't include in the list of fundamental selection criteria because it wasn't assessed for all candidates. When we get to discussions of developing and deploying talent, we need to fully explore learning agility, but it also bears mentioning here. Learning agility is the ability to transfer what's learned in one experience to other experiences. It sounds simple, but it's actually a fairly complex construct that's well supported by research. We embraced the assessment and development of learning agility whole-heartedly because it is a primary predictor of leadership capability to drive innovation and change.

Each of the dimensions above is useful for making predictions about talent. Each explains some amount of the variance between successful employees and unsuccessful employees. Taken together, they reveal a lot of the big picture. When it concerns the likelihood of an individual being successful in taking on new challenges or going into an unfamiliar role, there is no more powerful predictor than learning agility. For general managers, learning agility is essential. As people advance in their careers and roles become more complex, ambiguous, and subject to stress, learning agility increases in importance. For our high potential generalists, we devoted a full interview to assessing learning agility.

Exercise patience in selection

One final thought about recruiting. Over the years, I learned a lot about attracting and selecting talent. One of the most difficult lessons I had to learn was the need for patience. I'm not a patient man by nature. I could feel myself getting pissed this morning while standing in the buffet line at breakfast. Why in the hell do people have to stand and stare at the food? Don't study it. Just stick a fork in something, throw it on your plate, and move on!

Intellectually, I know that there's a time to exercise patience, and believe it or not, I do take pains to work on it. But if I'm honest, most of the time I don't view patience as a virtue. In fact, I can make a case that all progress in this world is due to impatient people. Don't get me started on slow drivers in the fast lane.

My impatience was a problem earlier in my career when I often found myself anxious to fill a key position and tempted to short-circuit the rigorous process we'd developed to select talent. When I did rush the process, it invariably came back and bit me on the ass. I eventually learned to be patient, and I'd encourage you to make time for recruiting so you can really do it well. Hiring the right people is one of your most important responsibilities as a leader.

Aligning Talent

Day 3: January 1st, Caribbean Sea

Last night Betsy informed me I had to wear a coat and tie to the New Year's Eve dinner and festivities. I dressed without complaining but was chafing at the tie and thinking, "Vacation my ass!" But dinner turned out to be interesting, and I quickly forgot my irritation with the dress requirements.

Whether by chance or, as I suspect, by design of the cruise director, we were seated at a dinner table with two other retired CEOs. Saul was accompanied by his spouse, but Robert appeared to be traveling solo, and I suspect the cruise director saw a potential match with Carol, my sister-in-law, who was also in attendance. In case I forgot to mention, my dear wife had shown foresight and a deep understanding of my predilections by inviting Carol on the cruise so she'd have someone to accompany her to the onboard musical theater, spa, and shops while sparing me the agony of doing so.

The two retired CEOs couldn't have been more different. Saul informed us he had been in the printing and direct mail business in New Jersey but now lived in Florida and was consumed with his real passion, horse racing. He was, not to put too fine a point on it, a cretin. He had poor table manners, interrupted others frequently, and generally dominated the conversation with stories of his racing stable.

In direct contrast, Robert was gracious, showed interest in others, and asked good questions when there was an opening in the conversation, that is, when Saul briefly stopped yammering to swill his scotch. Robert had retired as CEO of a global chemical company and had a long, successful career, mostly with one company. He told us he recently lost his wife and that he'd been invited by his three sons to join with their families on the cruise. He said it was a great opportunity to spend some quality time with his kids and grandkids, and that made me pause and make a mental note to spend some time later on shopping with my wife, which, for her, might be the epitome of quality time.

Robert's career and CEO experience are undoubtedly very different than mine. I asked him what three recommendations he'd make to a young person who aspired to become CEO. Without hesitation Robert offered up three constructive suggestions.

"First, set realistic expectations. Only a few people ever get a shot at the top job, and those who do probably don't have a career plan that went the way they anticipated. Many current CEOs never dreamed when younger that they'd become a CEO one day. I'd tell a young person to expect the unexpected. If you're really good at what you do, you're going to be given challenges for which you're unprepared and assignments you don't want. Accept those challenges because that's where the most learning happens. It's paying your dues, part of the high price you pay to get to the corner office."

At this point Saul interrupted by reaching across Robert's plate to grab the butter. Not so much as an "Excuse me."

Once the butter plate cleared, Robert continued, "Second, become absolutely the best at a few really important things and pretty good at everything else. You absolutely have to understand your weaknesses and deal with every one of them. You can't afford any flaws that will derail you. That's hard work and also part of the price to be paid."

Another interruption from Saul, this time as he unsuccessfully tried to hide a belch and then remarked, "Damn cucumbers."

Betsy could sense I was about to say something and gave my leg a slight squeeze under the table. Rather than tell Saul that he should try chewing his food, I just gave Robert a knowing look and asked him to go on.

"And third," Robert continued, "surround yourself with good people and get the most from them. I've seen quite a few passed over for the top job because they didn't have the people skills. And I've seen a few derail along the way because of people issues."

Robert's suggestions weren't exactly revelations for me at this point in my life, but I expect I would have found them very useful when starting my career in business. I've related them here because they lend credibility to several of the lessons I want to address ahead, and his third suggestion about getting the most out of your people provides a nice segue into my next topic of aligning talent.

Previously I shared my views about attracting and selecting the best talent for your organization. Of course, talent management doesn't stop with hiring. You have to integrate talent into your organization and accelerate their speed to performance so they're contributing as soon as possible. Beyond that, you need to keep them engaged, provide ongoing development, and deploy them into jobs to meet your business needs and build a talent pipeline that will meet future needs.

For now, let's focus on the integration and alignment of talent, which is primarily done through two practices: onboarding and performance management. They're both important, but performance management overshadows onboarding and just about every other talent management practice. It is one of the most difficult practices to get right. When done well, the positive impact on the business is huge. But when done poorly, the negative impact can be devastating. There's no one right way to do performance management, but there are definitely some wrong ways. I'll share what's worked for me, but first, a few thoughts about onboarding.

Value of rigorous onboarding

Onboarding is a structured process to quickly integrate new employees into the organization and into their role so they start on the right foot, quickly begin contributing, and understand how to support the organization's values. Onboarding aligns the new employee with the goals of the team and norms of team behavior. Onboarding will provide answers to the likely questions of new employees:

≈ *Regarding deliverables:* What are my deliverables? How are my deliverables measured? How do my deliverables impact my team and the broader organization? Etc.

≈ *Regarding people:* Who are the people with whom I need to be familiar? With whom should I be personally acquainted? Who can answer key questions? Who can make key decisions? Who can provide me with resources I need? Etc.

༠ *Regarding tools, facilities, procedures:*
Where's my workstation? The restroom? The
cafeteria? When do I get paid? How do I enroll in
benefits? How do I submit an expense report? What
tools or applications do I need? How do I use them?
Etc.

༠ *Regarding organizational culture:* What does
this organization really value? What are examples
and non-examples of related behavior? What
generally surprises new employees about working
here? What gets people in trouble around here?
What's the organizational history? What are the
legends of successes and failures? Etc.

Onboarding milestones

Our approach to onboarding was to convene a volunteer
team of emerging high potentials—highly regarded
employees who had been with the company for less
than five years—to design the process with some
limited guidance. Working together, they generated a
comprehensive list of questions such as those above and
linked each question to one of the following time periods:

༠ Before the first day on the job

༠ First day on the job

༠ First week on the job

༠ First month on the job

༠ First quarter on the job

From that, they created a job aid for hiring managers, a checklist of sorts, addressing what needed to be done to onboard the new hire including the questions to be answered, when, and by whom. As soon as an offer was accepted, HR sent the job aid with related information to the hiring manager, IT, security, and others who needed information. They also had an app that automatically set up a series of calendar reminders that would pop up to make sure the hiring manager had no excuse for forgetting an onboarding step. Every new employee was assigned two buddies, one from their own department and another from a different department, and each buddy had responsibility to provide particular information and answer questions.

I don't believe you can learn anything unless you have an opportunity to practice and to make mistakes. To learn, you need opportunities to fail. We made quite a few mistakes in onboarding before we got it right.

Once I noticed an employee I didn't recognize sitting at his desk reading a novel on a Friday afternoon. Curious, I stopped and introduced myself. Clinton dropped his novel, embarrassed, and informed me that he'd started earlier that week but was waiting to receive direction from his boss who was on vacation until Monday. He said he'd read through the employee handbook several times and was anxious to get started, but he didn't know what else to do until his boss returned. Believe me. Then and there I gave Clinton some specific direction, and on Monday I did the same with Clinton's boss.

Here's a summary of lessons learned about onboarding:

≈ *Before start date.* Onboarding needs to begin well before the start date. That's when lots of information is generated and provided to the candidate, the hiring manager, and others. You want to make sure you've provided enough information to candidates that they feel prepared and confident when they walk through the door on their first day. You also need to attend to setting up a workstation, installing computer programs, preparing payroll and security documents for signature, etc.

It's inexcusable to be unprepared for the arrival of a new employee. Inexcusable! The first day is incredibly important.

There was a time we were especially concerned about unanticipated turnover, concerned about good employees who chose to leave. We began doing exit interviews in an attempt to understand why good employees left. At first, we typically got muted responses to our open-ended questions about reasons for leaving. Answers generally referred in rather vague terms to another opportunity or a personal situation, but we weren't convinced we were getting to the root causes.

After trial and error, we developed a set of closed-ended questions that addressed their onboarding experience, level of engagement, and cultural fit. These questions complemented open-ended questions in the exit interview. We found it easy to modify the exit interview and use it to conduct "stay" interviews with key talent on a periodic basis.

I'm mentioning the exit interview now because one of the questions we asked was, "When did you first begin to think you would not have a long-term future with our company?" The answers astounded us—well over 50% said in the first month, and a surprisingly large percentage said they had doubts on their first day! That kind of data will make you sit up and pay attention to onboarding.

≈ *First day.* If the period before the start date is important in the onboarding process, the first day is crucial. It was a requirement in our firm for the hiring manager to be on hand to welcome the employee when they arrived and to spend the first 30 minutes in a welcome conversation before they were handed off to HR.

After signing forms, receiving benefits information, getting a security badge, etc., HR handed off the new hire to their in-department buddy who spent the remainder of the morning helping them get introduced to their team and acquainted with their workspace. Lunch was with the manager. The first part of the afternoon was spent with the alternate buddy. We gave them the last couple of hours of the first workday to get acclimated in ways that varied with their position. If for any reason the hiring manager was unable to greet the employee or have lunch with the candidate, the boss's boss filled in.

≈ *Detailed plan.* Scripting the entire onboarding process is very important, and we filled the first week pretty extensively with get-acquainted meetings with coworkers who were important to the role being filled. Each month I did a 30-minute personal welcome for all employees who had joined in the past 30 days. It was always a casual and cozy setting, and even as we grew in size, we rarely had more than 20 new employees in any given month. I remember, though, in the early days there was a month in which we only had one new employee, but I conducted the CEO welcome just the same.

We found that without a detailed script that specifically assigned actions and a schedule, things would slip. We audited this process by surveying new hires after 100 days to gauge how well we were following the plan and to solicit ideas that could help us enhance the process.

Onboarding senior talent

We found, perhaps counterintuitively, that onboarding was more critical for senior positions, but without special effort, was less likely to be done rigorously. The senior person will be quick on the uptake and likely impatient with a drawn-out onboarding process. That encourages shortcuts.

Rather than just take shortcuts, we changed the process somewhat for senior positions. We accelerated the basics, e.g., we didn't feel it necessary to give senior new hires a guided tour so they could find the restroom, but we spent more time on both the cultural perspective and the overall business perspective, e.g., customers, competition, industry, revenue model, etc.

Also, for senior people we implemented a "first impressions" 360 evaluation after only 30 days. I suppose this type of assessment is a violation of best practice that states people should be on the job for a full year before receiving a 360, but I was willing to experiment. It's a crappy feeling to invest so much time and energy in selecting the right candidate only to have them derail in the first year (remember Jeff?).

I engaged a coach to debrief the 360s and identify potential derailment issues. The data and content of coaching conversations were kept confidential, but employees were encouraged to have a follow-up meeting with their boss to discuss what was learned. I personally had several of these meetings, and I believe we prevented derailment of several good people through this practice.

In one case, I had a senior process engineer, Rajani, who got off on the wrong foot and had managed to alienate his colleagues almost immediately. He was clueless until he received feedback. Following some coaching, Rajani met individually with each of his peers, acknowledged his missteps, and asked for help and support. He made a complete turnaround and became one of our most respected engineers. If our first-impression 360s saved one Rajani, they were worth the effort.

That's enough said about onboarding. It's not rocket science, but it does take some planning and a focus on execution. Done well, onboarding will improve employee retention and accelerate performance.

Why performance management is so critical

Performance management is also about employee retention and accelerating performance—and so much more. If you can only do one talent management process right, make it performance management.

When done well, performance management will enhance employee engagement, shape your organizational culture to reflect the values you want, and align employees to your strategic intent. When done well, performance management optimizes performance and will positively impact every key performance indicator for your business. Quality. Productivity. Sales revenue. Customer loyalty. Retention of your most valued employees. Every key performance indicator!

On the other hand, if you screw it up, performance management will alienate your best employees, destroy morale, and kill your business results. Done poorly, performance management will create a toxic organizational culture. In fact, performance management is probably the most powerful driver of your organizational culture.

If I was given one hour to assess your organization's culture, I'd spend it asking a cross-section of employees about how you do performance management. I would learn about how expectations are set, how feedback is given, your rewards strategy, how you deal with conflict, how you manage problem performers, your approach to recognition, the quality of your managers, and probably how you terminate people.

How is it possible to learn so much from examining one organizational practice? Because performance management encompasses the fundamentals of managing people, and people are the primary drivers of organizational performance and culture.

Management is about setting expectations, giving direction, providing feedback and coaching, reinforcing desired behavior, correcting undesired behavior, recognizing achievements, and differentiating people so we can appropriately differentiate their development, deployment, and rewards. Management is about doing all these things so that individually and collectively we achieve optimum results. That's what your managers are paid to do. And because too often they don't, performance management has evolved.

Simply put, performance management is a lame attempt to get managers to be responsible and do their job.

The generic description of performance management goes something like this... Performance management is a process that starts with goal setting at the beginning of a business year. Each employee has performance goals that are the basis for feedback and coaching which is done formally in a mid-year review. At the end of the business year, performance is reviewed and assessed against achievement of goals. The employee receives a final rating, which feeds into compensation decisions.

Why performance management (almost always) stinks

OK, got it? Sounds simple enough. So what's wrong with this process? Why do your managers and employees hate it so much? They do, you know. There are a lot of reasons. Here are a few:

> ≋ *It's driven by compliance.* As soon as metrics are established and monitored for compliance, managers begin to view their goal as completion of a task, checking off a box to be in compliance. Yes, I set goals with my employees. Check. Yes, I did my mid-year reviews. Check. Yes, all my employees have a development plan. Check.
>
> This mindset is noxious because it ignores the primary objective of performance management, which is to have frequent, meaningful conversations

between boss and employee. If the boss and employee are having frequent, meaningful conversations, it's likely there will be clear expectations, feedback, coaching, and differentiation.

If meaningful conversations aren't occurring, checking off boxes only serves to annoy managers because it's recognized as the waste of time it is. It annoys employees who know when they're being short-changed. And it annoys HR because they're usually cast in the role of performance management police to ensure compliance. In the end, checking off boxes for the sake of compliance doesn't improve a damn thing. It probably makes things worse.

≋ *Goals change.* Business is dynamic. Requirements change. Goals are sometimes outdated within a month of being written. If frequent conversations aren't occurring, the specifics of goals tend to be forgotten until it's time for the mid-year or, worse, end-of-year review. At that point, the manager is stuck because it doesn't make sense to evaluate obsolete goals that were set six months or a year ago. The employee feels screwed, and rightly so.

≋ *Managers generally lack skill.* Managers aren't skilled in providing feedback and coaching. To get good at something, you need to practice. Just ask anyone who excels at his game, whether it's a karate black belt, a grandmaster chess player, or an exemplary welder. It's extremely rare to find a manager who ever considers making time to practice the skills of providing feedback and coaching. If managers aren't having frequent, meaningful conversations, they're not getting practice.

As a general rule, we tend to like things that we do well and dislike things we do poorly. It's unlikely you like to bowl if you suck at bowling. Since managers, by and large, are ineffective coaches, they vigorously dislike giving feedback. And employees are understandably unhappy about having Bozo the ass-clown for a boss and supposed coach.

≋ *Managers lack a performance vocabulary.* You can't have a meaningful conversation about performance without a comprehensive vocabulary to describe performance. It's ineffectual to speak in general terms. "Nice job." "You need to raise your game." "Do better." It's like trying to have the sex talk with your pre-pubescent child without knowing the terminology. Without a precise, behaviorally anchored vocabulary, managers will have an aversion to performance conversations and employees are short-changed.

≋ *Managers have big egos.* There are many explanations for why managers don't have frequent, meaningful conversations, and I believe unchecked egos are at the root of many of them. Meaningful conversations place the manager's ego at risk. Egos lead managers to prioritize their own agenda over having meaningful conversations. When conversations do occur, the manager's ego gets the focus rather than the employee and the issues at hand. Egos lead managers to protect their desired image, to sacrifice courage for popularity. Egos promote subjectivity over objectivity, exacerbate biases, and make it difficult to differentiate. As long as managers lack the emotional intelligence to subjugate their ego, meaningful conversations—and employees—will suffer.

≈ *Compensation gets in the way.* Performance management is inextricably and directly linked to compensation. When conversations are infrequent, formal, and documented (as in mid-year and end-of-year reviews), the link to compensation overshadows everything else for the employee. It's nearly impossible to have a meaningful conversation about performance when the employee is on pins and needles and only thinking about how their rating will impact their compensation.

≈ *Problems compound to sink the process.* Virtually everyone knows when the whole thing is a sham. And all too often it is. Performance ratings are a joke. They don't really differentiate. When marginal employees receive pretty much the same ratings and pay increases as good employees, it's a particularly bitter pill for your top performers. People just try to get through the goal-setting phase, check off the box, and then get on with their real work. Feedback is rare and generally negative. Meaningful conversations with the boss? Forget it. When it's time for the review, goals get dusted off and stress skyrockets in anticipation of the dreaded performance appraisal.

Perhaps you're in one of those one-out-of-a-hundred organizations in which performance management is done flawlessly and universally revered. If so, I'm glad for you. In my attempt to become one of those organizations, I tried just about every performance management variation at one time or another. Highly structured goals. Cascaded goals. Optional goals. Mid-year reviews. Quarterly reviews. Peer reviews. Forced ratings. Forced rankings. No ratings. Mandated development plans. And so on. We continued to experiment until we found the combination that worked for us.

Our approach to performance management

Our employees probably found the continuous experimentation frustrating, but at least they knew we were genuinely interested in doing the right thing and not just trying to check off boxes. It's not likely that our approach will fit every other organization in every way. There are lessons we learned, though, that are worthy of consideration, and I offer them here to be helpful rather than to preach a dogma.

≈ *Goal setting.* We found it impossible to define specific goal criteria that worked for everyone. Applying the SMART acronym (i.e., some variation of specific, measureable, actionable, realistic, and time-based) works better for some roles than others. Some goals pretty much stand alone and can't be easily cascaded or defined as a component of a higher-level team or organizational goal. Expectations for some employees are stable and fully described by the context of the job. For those employees it's nonsensical and artificial to create goals that don't do any more than reiterate the job description.

For these reasons and as a way to encourage managers to be responsible, we left it up to individual managers to decide if, when, and how their employees would set goals. Our guideline to managers was simple and consisted of four parts:

1. Make it absolutely clear to every employee what they're expected to deliver of value.

2. Describe to every employee how work should be done using both positive and negative examples.

3. Explain to every employee how their deliverables impact the team and organization.

4. Adjust the bar as required so no one can meet expectations while coasting.

≈ *Performance coaching.* Some meaningful conversations are forward-looking and developmental in nature. Our managers generally found these conversations easy to do. They found it much more difficult to do performance coaching, to have conversations that looked backward and discussed what was delivered, how it was delivered, and the impact on the team.

I did my best to model performance coaching and expected my managers to follow suit. We invested in developing this skill in our managers, and training consisted of practicing coaching conversations, especially difficult conversations that required the coach to address disagreement, defensiveness, and conflict. Managers took turns scoring each other on how well they demonstrated good feedback and coaching techniques. Before long, they felt much more comfortable, and we elevated coaching skills across the board.

Our scorecard assessed how well managers did these nine things:

1. Provided feedback that was timely, specific, authentic, and direct

2. Modified their approach to fit the employee

3. Described the impact of performance
4. Addressed obstacles to performance
5. Checked their ego
6. Demonstrated managerial courage
7. Gave helpful guidance for course correction
8. Provided appropriate reinforcement
9. Kept the tone constructive

We created a Performance Coaching Guide for managers to support the training. Developing and reinforcing this skill in our management ranks was the centerpiece of our performance management process because it was the greatest enabler of meaningful conversations, the ultimate goal. Our expectation was that managers have very frequent conversations and document significant conversations and issues as deemed appropriate.

≈ *Development coaching.* As previously stated, managers found development conversations relatively easy to do, but that doesn't mean they naturally made development a priority. We tried but abandoned the typical approach of requiring employees to annually complete a development plan. We abandoned that practice because we found that forced development plans were unnecessary for motivated learners and viewed as a chore—just a box to be checked—by those who weren't self-motivated.

We decided a pull rather than a push strategy would be more effective in creating and reinforcing the desired learning culture. The only thing we asked our managers was that they have a formal developmental conversation with each employee at least once per year. Documentation was encouraged but not required. Employees were encouraged but not required to create a development plan.

Our approach was to reinforce and celebrate the behavior we wanted. Our monthly employee newsletter had a section, the Development Corner, which highlighted achievements of employees and explicitly described how achievements were linked to development goals that had been discussed with managers. We celebrated accomplishments in other ways; managers even had discretion to award spot bonuses—more on this a few points down.

In addition to promoting self-development by our employees, we prepared managers to effectively do development coaching in much the same way we addressed performance coaching.

Managers were taught to do the following:

1. Understand career motivations
2. Assess development needs of employees
3. Plan opportunities for developing targeted competencies on the job
4. Provide reinforcement and recognition for demonstrated growth
5. Address negative behaviors as required
6. Provide guidance on appropriate development strategies
7. Create effective development plans
8. Facilitate learning from others
9. Track development progress

10. Understand and describe key jobs in the organization

11. Speak knowledgeably about the nature of careers in the organization

12. Avoid making promises they couldn't keep

Learning means acquiring the ability to do something new. You can't separate learning from behavior, and behavior is temporary if not practiced and reinforced with positive consequences. One of the most important responsibilities of our managers was to provide consequences so what employees learned would stick.

≋ *Performance appraisal.* Most organizations do performance appraisals because of the perceived benefit to the organization. It's believed that an appraisal will be a valuable cover-your-ass documentation if an employee challenges a termination decision. That's a mistake. Performance appraisals, because they're done poorly, actually benefit the discharged employee nine times out of ten. Performance appraisals done to justify compensation decisions are for the benefit of the organization, not the employee.

When we pursued appraisals for these reasons, we damaged employee engagement and there was a net negative impact on the organization, so we changed. Our decision was to consider appraisals from the employee perspective. As a result, we kept in place an annual formal performance review but eventually did away with a numerical scoring system. We had no single ratings for employees. No "Meets Expectations." No "Exceeds Expectations." Instead, our appraisals were narrative documents completed by both manager and employee with open text fields on each side of the document—one side for managers and the other side for employees.

Managers were expected to note major achievements and contributions made by the employee, and they were also provided behaviorally-anchored descriptors of performance that helped them populate their side of the document to describe how work was done. Employees could add anything they wanted to their side of the document. This approach removed a lot of the BS that occurred when managers felt they had to give a certain overall performance rating and then defend it during the performance review.

There's less subjectivity when you're describing actual achievements and using behaviorally-anchored statements to describe behaviors. These documents became running career histories of the contribution and growth of all our employees. They were helpful in shaping a constructive conversation and generally positively viewed by both managers and employees. They were also valuable reference documents during talent reviews.

One very important thing we learned was that it was not constructive to address compensation during the performance review. When we combined the performance review with informing employees about compensation decisions, it turned out that employees could focus on nothing else and managers mainly focused on justifying the comp decision instead of having a meaningful conversation that summarized the contribution and behaviors of the past year. Instead, we separated the comp decision by three months and had a separate discussion with employees at that time about merit increases.

≈ *Link to compensation.* Few would question the importance of linking performance to compensation, but it's easier said than done. I'll address compensation here as it relates to performance management and again when we address employee engagement.

Because I had a keen interest to create a true meritocracy, a high performance culture, I instituted a pay-for-performance strategy. At first, we had problems because it encouraged some undesired behaviors. For example, we had some employees who, in an attempt to bolster their compensation, operated too independently. Selfishly. Eventually, we created a model that included an assessment of individual, team, and organizational performance in the determination of compensation.

We developed broad salary bands and were transparent about related salary ranges and how they applied to various career paths. Initially, our process was for managers to submit recommendations to HR, who would make the final annual comp decisions. The problem with this approach was that it took accountability away from managers and opened up the door for them to tell employees that final pay decisions were out of their hands.

Instead, we empowered line managers to make pay decisions (except related to long-term incentives for senior employees) within budgetary limits and certain guidelines, which included the salary bands. Budgets for each manager were determined by a combination of organizational performance and an evaluation of the team; a significant portion of the annual end-of-year budget for comp increases was earmarked for variable compensation rather than cost-of-living.

Managers were given guidance to make modest adjustments to base comp to address cost-of-living and changes in movement within grade. They had discretion to provide variable comp in the form of cash bonuses that did not impact base comp. There was also a modest, dedicated variable comp budget that gave them some flexibility to provide spot bonuses throughout the year.

Managers received instruction and a guide (generic representation below) to help them distribute their comp budget to reward performance. At first, they resisted this quite a bit because it made them accountable and required some extra work on their part.

For the first couple of years, many managers sought help from HR, but that number dropped off significantly after they'd been through a couple of comp cycles. Of course, they were always free to consult HR for guidance, but in the end they accepted responsibility for this and were much more engaged in talent differentiation. They found it a huge advantage to separate the performance appraisal from the salary discussion.

Performance Rating	Lower third of band	Middle third of band	Upper third of band
Elite Performers	$$$$ base + $$$ variable	$$$ base + $$$ variable	$$ base + $$$ variable
Distinctive Performers	$$$ base + $$ variable	$$ base + $$ variable	$ base + $$ variable
Solid Performers	$$ base + $ variable	$ base + $ variable	0 base + $ variable
Marginal Performers	0 base + 0 variable	0 base + 0 variable	0 base + 0 variable

≋ *Manager support.* I've already briefly described the development and support we provided managers so they could effectively provide performance and development coaching. But we did more. Early on, I struggled with the role HR should play in performance management. We quickly moved away from the compliance focus in which HR functioned as the performance management police, but managers still looked to HR as the voice of authority and ultimate accountability for performance management. This wasn't in line with my idea of a performance culture, and we addressed it in a couple of ways.

We decided to create a cadre of internal performance management consultants from our pool of emerging high potentials. They were volunteers who saw the role as rewarding job enrichment and a developmental opportunity. Each consultant was assigned a handful of managers and served as the first line of support to answer questions about performance coaching, development, performance appraisal, etc.

This turned out to be a great tactic. It freed up HR to be more strategic and to leverage the education they provided for our young high potentials volunteers who got a great development experience in the bargain. Ultimately, we had a capable HR function facilitating performance management, but managers were the real owners.

≈ *Evaluating the performance management process.* We experimented with quite a few metrics in our attempt to evaluate our performance management process. Most of the measures initially considered were quantitative in nature (e.g., participation rates for annual development coaching), and we found that all metrics we tried that were purely quantitative in nature tended to support the notion of compliance and checking boxes rather than to drive meaningful conversations.

Through trial and error, we developed a rather simple approach to evaluation that incorporated qualitative metrics. We used a stratified random sampling process to select a small number of employees to survey every other month. One of the HR staff administered a quick phone survey to 10-15 employees and entered verbatim responses in a data collection form in real time. We just asked three questions:

1. Can you please tell me about the most helpful conversation you've had with your boss in the past month or so?

2. Can you please tell me your number one work priority right now and why it's so important?

3. If you could sit down with your boss right now to have a conversation, what would you like to discuss and why?

If a survey on a particular team revealed some potential problems, we'd sample a couple more from the pertinent group to see if there was indeed a theme that needed to be addressed. It only required about a half day six times per year from the HR staff to provide me with very useful data.

No employee names were associated with responses, but I was able to see the team and manager associated with comments and followed up with individual managers to provide reinforcement when there was evidence of effective conversations. I also sanitized statements to ensure they wouldn't be linked to a respondent and used them with broader audiences to provide positive and negative examples of behavior we desired.

It all comes down to meaningful conversations

Once I participated in a meeting with the single objective of deciding on the rating scale we'd use in our performance appraisal. Shall we have a four-point or a five-point rating scale? Should we label our mid-point as Meets Performance or Acceptable Performance? We spent a full afternoon on this trivial crap. Four hours!

I don't think we're unusual. Many organizations focus on the trivial when designing their performance management process. Four-point vs. five-point rating scale. Meets Performance vs. Acceptable Performance. All such considerations are a waste of time. Will the answer to either of these questions change the nature of conversations between managers and employees? If not, don't waste your time. Move on. Your focus should be on implementing practices that promote frequent, meaningful conversations.

After some false starts, we got there. We created a high performance culture by focusing on conversations rather than compliance. In doing so, we simplified and removed the pain from performance management.

Engaging Talent

Day 4: January 2nd, Caribbean Sea

The first couple of days on board the ship, I was restless. Actually, it was a little more than that. I was stressed and impatient for the cruise to be over. But yesterday afternoon we stopped at a port so my fellow passengers and I could disembark, stretch our legs, and celebrate the New Year by injecting some cash into the local island economy.

The stop did provide me with a welcome diversion. While Betsy and my sister-in-law did their part in boosting the fortunes of local vendors of souvenirs and jewelry, I rented a bicycle and pedaled until I found a pub with some spicy shredded pork, local rum, and local color.

Pork and rum and banter with the natives put me in a good mood, and my stress relief was complete when, upon leaving the pub, I saw my bike was still leaning against the tree where I'd left it. A kid, probably ten-years-old, was standing beside it, one hand on the handlebars. He had a can of shoe polish and a ratty old rag in his free hand, which struck me as odd since not a person on the island, including visiting tourists, was wearing leather shoes.

The kid's smile was dazzling. He introduced himself as Miguel Angelo and promptly informed me that he had dedicated the last hour to shining up my bike and guarding it with a vigilance that would shame a Doberman guard dog.

Miguel Angelo's entrepreneurship and persistence were truly inspirational. I'd left my cowboy boots behind on the ship in favor of sneakers, and it quickly became clear that I didn't have anything else for him to shine up with his rag, so he fervently pitched his skills as a tour guide. I told him that if he had a bike, I might take him up on the offer. Turns out that wasn't a problem for Miguel Angelo. I rode slowly, and he ran alongside my bike for nearly an hour pointing out the local landmarks, which mostly consisted of banana and breadfruit trees.

When we got back to the cruise ship, he asked for five bucks. I gave him twenty. In response, he insisted I take a silver coin, local currency, to keep as a memento. His gesture seemed sincere, quite touching, actually. Miguel Angelo made a deep impression on me. He had energy and enthusiasm and style. I admired his spunk. He was fully engaged in his enterprise. He really owned it. Miguel Angelo gave me inspiration for today's topic.

The sense of ownership displayed by young Miguel Angelo is at the centerpiece of the engagement mindset. Entrepreneurs are engaged by definition. Entrepreneurs are invested in their enterprise, financially invested, but more importantly, psychologically invested.

As an entrepreneur, I've rarely felt relaxed. Never been fully rested. Never felt contented. But even when working for someone else, I've always felt like an owner.

My sense of ownership is a defining characteristic. It's made me happy, and that's different from feeling contented or satisfied. Ownership never allowed me to be satisfied with our level of business success. Ownership drove me to never be satisfied with myself. And please don't give me any crap about accepting myself or "I'm OK, you're OK" hokum.

Good mental health does not imply you've arrived. It means you're OK with your journey. Ownership gave me that—constructive dissatisfaction with the current state of my business and my personal development but proud and happy to be on a journey of my choosing. That's what ownership means to me.

For 30 years I worked hard to instill a sense of ownership in my workforce, to fully engage my employees. Engaged employees feel a sense of ownership, and that makes them loyal to you and to the business. It compels them to willingly do more than the minimum, to do more than is expected. Ownership gives them a sense of responsibility that directs their efforts so they're aligned with your strategy. And, importantly, a sense of ownership leads them to stay with you.

In fact, there are really only two ways to retain top talent: 1) bribe them, or 2) engage them. I chose engagement.

Engagement defined

To put it in one sentence: Engagement is a mindset in which your employees feel a personal sense of ownership, and that mindset leads them to be loyal, to willingly work harder than they need to work, to focus their work on what matters, and to stay with you.

If you buy that, then the value of engagement should be patently obvious. That mindset leads to behaviors that drive virtually every business metric that matters. Increasing engagement will enhance revenue, profit, customer loyalty, quality, and innovation. Increasing engagement will drive down tardiness, absenteeism, accidents, theft, and employee turnover.

I think I always intuitively understood the value of engagement, but I didn't always appreciate the difference between engagement and happiness. As an owner, I didn't always feel rested or relaxed. I was never contented with my achievements, but I always had an underlying happiness. Early on I made the mistake made by many organizations—I confused engagement with contentment.

Engagement is not satisfaction. Engagement is not contentment. If contented cows give better milk, you might think that contented employees do better work. Nope. Not necessarily true. In fact, you may find yourself wishing some of your contented employees would leave and go join a contented herd at a competitor's business.

About engagement

Here's a summary of what I've learned about employee engagement.

   ≋ *Engagement matters.* Businesses that do not proactively work on engagement are ignorant, apathetic, or sadly misguided. There are many drivers of business success. Employee engagement is one of the biggest, too big to ignore.

   ≋ *Engagement is not about happiness or satisfaction.* It is about ownership and a sense of responsibility. It pays to understand the difference and to make sure all your managers understand it too. It's inaccurate to say that engaged employees are always happy—usually they are, but not always. But more importantly, it's also inaccurate to say that happy employees are always engaged—very often they are not.

≈ *Seeking only to make employees happy rather than engaged is a fool's errand.* There are companies that spend lots of money and energy to be listed as one of a handful of companies that are wonderful places to work. For many of these companies (not all), it appears the factors described as qualifying criteria are primarily related to tangible benefits and perks. Everyone likes benefits. You can buy benefits. In that sense, I guess you may be able to buy a measure of happiness. But happiness is not engagement. You cannot buy engagement. It's nice to have happy employees. It's enormously valuable to have engaged employees.

≈ *The relationship between engagement and business success is a two-way causal loop.* This is critical to understand. In one direction, engagement—by definition—helps drive business success. As engagement increases, your business will benefit in every key performance indicator. But it's not just a one-direction relationship. You'll also find that as your business improves (especially as it grows), it naturally raises engagement.

Cause and effect works both ways. This is a good news/bad news situation. Imagine two organizations that are equivalent in every way except in their challenges related to growth. Organization One is growing due to favorable market conditions and finds that engagement naturally increases—which in turn is likely to stimulate more growth. They experience an upward, self-reinforcing spiral. Organization Two is in a stagnant market and losing ground. It will find engagement levels falling even though the way they deal with the workforce is identical to the first organization. In the worst case,

Organization Two can find itself in a downward death spiral.

The fact is that we all like to play on a winning team. If you're winning in the marketplace, you'll find it much easier to drive engagement and reap the rewards. Conversely, we hate to lose. Most of us hate to lose even more than we like to win. And if you're losing in the marketplace, your work is cut out for you. You have an uphill battle, but you also have all the more reason to focus on engagement.

Realize that the way you define winning is probably not the way your employees define it. Somewhere in your definition of winning is a dollar sign. You can be making money hand-over-fist, but if you're socking it away or returning it all to investors at the expense of growth, employees probably won't feel they're winning in the same way you do. Your employees care about growth. Growth means action. Growth means movement. Growth means opportunity. For employees, if you're not growing, you're not winning.

≈ *You can drive engagement, but you never arrive.* There are a number of vendors that have engagement research, assessments, and normative data. A valid and reliable instrument that assesses loyalty, energy, and retention will give you an engagement score, an indication of the engagement health of your employee population. It's useful to measure engagement every year or two so you can track your progress.

Personally, I didn't find a lot of value in normative data that allowed me to compare my company's engagement with industry averages. Part of my job as CEO was to create a sense of urgency for change and improvement, and norms didn't make that job easier when we were scoring above industry averages. I preferred for us to set our own bar, to compete against ourselves. And that's what we did. We tracked our progress from year to year at the organization and department levels. Department managers set goals, tracked their progress, and were accountable for continuously enhancing engagement.

Drivers of engagement

It's one thing to know your degree of healthiness. It's another thing to know what will make you healthier. It's valuable to know your engagement score, but it's even more valuable to know how capable you are in driving engagement. Select an instrument that will help you understand your organization's capability in the drivers of engagement, including boss relationships, strategic alignment, confidence in leadership, employee development, and recognition and rewards.

An engagement driver is a lever that enables you to lift engagement. It took me a while to learn how to wield the levers, and teaching my managers to wield them effectively was a never-ending process. I found that some drivers were more important than others, at least in my organization. It's likely that the drivers I found to be most important will also be important for you, but there may be differences between organizations based on industry or culture.

For instance, employee development is an important driver, a universal driver. If you provide suitable development opportunities, employees will be more likely engaged regardless of industry. That said, it's a pretty safe bet that in most organizations staffed with well educated, credentialed professionals, development will be a relatively powerful driver. In organizations staffed primarily with unskilled workers, employee development certainly matters, but other drivers may have higher relative value.

Engagement drivers vary in power at the organizational level, but they also vary in importance to individuals, and it's valuable to understand and respect those differences. Below are the engagement drivers I found most powerful and some methods I've learned to move those levers.

Strategic alignment drives engagement

Imagine you're taking your family on vacation across the country to San Diego. Before you leave, you sit down with the kids and tell them all about SeaWorld. You describe the Shamu Show, the water rides, and aquarium. You use vivid language. You show them pictures of other kids swimming with dolphins and kissing a whale. You take them on a virtual tour of the San Diego Zoo, the aerial tram, and the after-dark guided walk through the park. But you don't stop there. You show them pictures of the resort you've reserved for a week, the resort with a spa for your wife and daughter and golf course for you and your son.

And then, after creating the vision for them, you trace your route on a map to help set realistic expectations about the journey, not every detail, but the key milestones. You don't tell them that you're going to stop for gas in Yankton, but you tell them you're going to visit Mount Rushmore and spend a night in Rapid City. Assuming your kids like the vision you painted for them, they're likely to be pretty good traveling companions. They'll be engaged.

Now imagine another scenario in which your total pre-vacation communication consisted of terse instructions: "Get in the car. We're going west." You wouldn't be two hours from home before they'd be restless. By the end of the first day, you'd be battling a mutiny. Without buy-in to the destination and understanding of the required journey, they will be disengaged.

Now, I don't mean to insult employees by comparing them to our kids (or vice versa), but I do think this is an apt analogy. Just as a parent has a responsibility to help frame the future for the kids, leaders have a responsibility to frame the future for their employees. The destination is your vision, and the general route with milestones along the way is your strategy.

Your employees deserve to have a clear picture of your desired destination. They deserve to understand your vision. They need realistic expectations about the journey. They need to understand your strategy. If employees don't know where you're going and have realistic expectations about the journey, you can't expect them to be engaged. If they don't understand the route, you can't expect that their efforts will propel you in the right direction.

Strategic alignment has to start at the top with the CEO and senior leadership team. Every CEO assumes his or her team is fully aligned with the strategy. Do yourself a favor. Don't assume.

The senior team represents the pinnacle of strategic alignment in your organization. At every level, every team will be less aligned than the team above it, and the degree of misalignment will largely be determined by the level of alignment within the team above. It's like shooting a target at 25 yards with a short-barreled pistol. If your sights are misaligned just a very small fraction of an inch, you'll likely miss the target altogether. In the same way, any misalignment in the senior team is magnified at every level further down in the organization, and frontline employees may have little chance of being aligned. The senior team must get everything on the table and take the time to work through the issues. Don't quit before there's a strong sense of shared goals and precise alignment in the top team.

Every leader, starting with the CEO, should use clear, consistent, and vivid language to describe the vision and strategy. If you can't clearly describe the vision and strategy in about five minutes so it's understood by every employee, you need to revise your message. If you have financial metrics in your message, consider removing them. They don't count as strategy. "Twenty billion dollars by 2020" is a nice slogan, but it's not a strategy and it's not a vision for your employees.

For me, I wanted to let employees know where we were going to compete, what we needed to focus on to compete, and something about how we would compete. You might find my attempt at alliteration corny, but here is a summary of my ABC strategy presentation to employees:

A   *Where will we compete?*

*A*erospace. This is our Now. This is currently our primary market, and we are and will continue to be the dominant player in this market.

*A*utomotive. This is our Near Future. This is clearly an emerging market in which we will become the dominant player.

*A*dvanced Applications. This is our Far Future. We will aggressively participate in experimental technologies and with advanced applications to discover and create our future.

B How will we compete?

*B*reakneck Speed. We will advance with a speed that borders on recklessness. We will solve problems and innovate with a speed that amazes our customers and leaves our competitors in the dust. Our primary differentiator is our ability to provide practical and comprehensive solutions to our customers' problems with a speed that makes heads spin.

C What enables us to compete?

*C*ore Capabilities. We have unsurpassed expertise in composites materials science, tooling design, instrumentation, and specialized manufacturing processes. We will continuously and aggressively deepen our expertise in core capabilities. This is a driver of our ability to provide practical and comprehensive solutions from design to finished product.

*C*ore Values. We respect and reward innovation, initiative, and ingenuity. We are a meritocracy. We don't tolerate bureaucracy, mediocrity, or excuses. Those things will slow us down, and that's totally unacceptable. We are fast. We play to win. We love to win. We celebrate our wins. And we win faster than anyone.

*C*onquering Complexity. We are problem solvers first and foremost. The more complex the problem, the better. Complexity is our friend.

I covered these points virtually every time I addressed our employees but changed it up by providing different examples and non-examples to illustrate each point. Did you notice that there is no reference to sales revenue or profitability or any other financial metric? We had financial metrics, of course. They were important, and leaders were held accountable for our financial performance.

Our financial targets were not a secret. We shared financials with employees, and unless there was a compelling reason for confidentiality related to a joint venture, for instance, I was straightforward and answered any and all questions from employees about our finances.

In fact, I did my best to encourage those questions. We held an open employee forum at least once each month, and my CFO usually followed my strategy discussion with a financial overview. We answered any and all questions. Rather than shrink from tough questions from employees, we made a point of thanking the people who asked them. But I did not focus on financial goals when I spoke about strategy. I'm sure that seeing dollar signs in your strategy presentation makes your heart flutter. Your rank-and-file employees probably don't have the same reaction.

In addition to providing frequent and concise information about our vision and strategy, I insisted that every manager could answer three questions and teach these concepts to their teams:

1. Why do customers buy from us?

2. How do we make money?

3. How are we positioning ourselves in the competitive landscape?

I made a point of chatting about these topics with frontline employees whenever I had the chance and reinforced managers whose team members demonstrated a good understanding of our value proposition, business model, and strategy.

All the engagement drivers are important and meaningful to all employees. But some drivers are especially important to your high potential employees. Strategic alignment is one of those of particular concern to high potentials.

At the risk of stretching the analogy too far, I'd compare employees from the general population to your kids of grade-school age. They want to know where you're going on vacation and something about the journey, but your teenager with a learner's permit has an elevated level of interest. She might want to sit in the front seat and study the map. She will probably ask if she can drive part of the way. All your employees want to know about the vision and strategy. Your high potentials have to know.

Trustworthy and capable senior leaders drive engagement

OK, it's clear that employees are more engaged when they're strategically aligned, when they understand and support the destination and the nature of the journey. But it's not enough to know where the car is headed, they also want assurance that there's a competent driver behind the wheel.

If you've done a masterful job of creating and communicating your strategy, that's great. But you also need to back up your words. Your employees want to know they are following leaders who can capably execute the strategy.

Senior leaders who are respected and trustworthy drive engagement. And, of course, senior leaders perceived as indecisive, incapable, or deceitful destroy engagement. It's important for employees to get to know your senior leaders in order to develop trust and confidence in them.

If you don't provide opportunities for interactions, inaccurate reputations may be fabricated from thin air, inaccurate reputations that poison engagement. Ensure there's exposure to senior leaders so rank and file employees see how their leaders speak the truth, demonstrate personal integrity, and skillfully lead their teams.

No one needs to tell you if you have a leader—or any employee—who lies, cheats, or is chronically incompetent, you need get rid of him. Get rid of him now. Don't wait. Pull the trigger and then go back and review the selection criteria I wrote about a couple of days ago under recruiting talent.

Inspiring confidence in others requires more than just telling the truth and skillfully doing your job. This was driven home for me many years ago by Isabel, my young high potential that I assigned to the HR manager role.

One day after a staff meeting, Isabel, my newly promoted HR manager, knocked on my door and asked if I was open to some feedback. Well, who's going to say no to that question? Even while agreeing to feedback, I was feeling a sense of threat and had a rush of adrenaline. Like most everyone else who's asked that question, I was immediately on guard, my defense shield ready to deflect criticism with explanations and excuses.

Isabel said, "Barb had a good idea in the meeting, but you shot it down. I don't think you realize how you came across, and I thought you'd want to know." This launched us into an hour-long conversation about my leadership style.

The most uncomfortable truth might be most helpful

It was an uncomfortable conversation for me, and maybe I deserve a tiny bit of credit for seeing it through, but I can tell you it never would have happened if not for Isabel. For a young person, she was incredibly composed, mature… and ballsy. She was totally relaxed and focused on me and the situation. Her comfort level soon made me forget my discomfort, and I look back on that conversation as a turning point in my career. Here's the gist of what she shared with me:

- ≈ I was smart but liked to flaunt it. Without realizing it, I sometimes came across as arrogant and made other people feel stupid. I would appear a lot less arrogant if I'd stop to listen and show some interest in the ideas of others. She told me that no one was ever perceived as arrogant when they were listening or asking questions.

- ≈ I was a pretty good decision maker. But perhaps I wasn't as good as I thought I was. My self-confidence made me a poor listener and prevented me from getting input that would improve my decision making.

≋ I was impatient and fast, so fast that others had a hard time keeping up. I'd be able to see where I was losing people if I'd show some patience and stop once in a while long enough to listen. If I listened, perhaps I'd be able to bring them along.

≋ I was a perfectionist, and my desire for perfection made it difficult for me to hear anything that might be construed as criticism. The perfectionist streak gave me an outsized ego that might be balanced by demonstrating some humility. It didn't have to be difficult if I'd just: a) admit when I was wrong or when someone else knew more than I did and do so like it was no big deal; b) not take myself so seriously—laugh at myself once in a while: and, above all c) listen.

≋ I didn't realize how important it was for others to feel like their opinions mattered. Of course, opinions couldn't matter unless they were first heard. I needed to listen because it was important to others.

Do you see a theme here? Something about listening?

I'll never forget how Isabel summed it up. She told me that in the eyes of my employees, I was an unsympathetic Superman. She told me it would make all the difference if I'd balance Superman with Clark Kent, the mild-mannered reporter. I remember asking, "What in the hell are you talking about?"

Isabel told me that people want to follow a confident, capable leader, but they also want a leader who is human. I could deal with that paradox by taking a lesson from Clark

Kent. She told me a reporter asks questions, listens, and then creates stories about other people. Superman couldn't play the Clark Kent role simply by putting on a pair of glasses—that wouldn't fool anyone. He could only pass for Clark Kent by behaving like a mild-mannered reporter.

The meaning was clear. I needed to learn to check my ego (my kryptonite). I needed to take genuine interest in others, to ask questions, and, above all, to listen. Isabel told me that developing a Clark Kent alter-ego would round out my leadership style and make me a super CEO.

As hokey as all this probably sounds, it immediately made sense to me. I never gave Superman a run for his money, but I learned that by consciously and authentically adopting a Clark Kent persona when the situation called for it, I'd build trust and confidence in my employees.

This particular conversation with Isabel launched a career-long professional relationship that was profound and meaningful. My point in relating it here is that what I learned really impacted engagement. I learned that employees are engaged when they have confidence in senior leaders. I learned that integrity and technical competence are important, but it also takes listening and a dose of humility to build trust and inspire confidence. And I learned that I could model inspirational behaviors and coach others to do the same.

Employee development and career management drive engagement

These are big topics that I'll cover in some detail later, but here's a summary of what I've learned in relation to employee engagement:

- Acquiring the ability to do something new or to do something better is psychologically fulfilling and contributes to engagement. Proficiency is engaging. Conversely, lapses in confidence lead to dysfunctional behaviors and disengagement.

- It's nearly impossible to learn anything without the opportunity to fail. Persevering through failures in order to learn leads to psychological rewards and engagement. Fear of failure and prolonged attempts to learn without signs of success are both psychologically punishing and lead to disengagement.

- We learn most of what we need for success by doing a job. A job that is appropriately challenging and provides opportunity to learn and master new skills is engaging. A job that provides little or no challenge and no opportunity for failure is not developmental and fails to engage.

- An engaging career is more than a good job and decent paycheck. An engaging career represents long-term opportunity to continuously stretch and develop.

- Everyone has potential to learn and grow and improve, but everyone is not equal. We have different levels of motivation, different aptitudes, and different limitations in capabilities. We are not equally talented. We don't all provide equal value to our organizations. Equal treatment is not fair treatment.

  If you want to be fair and you want to optimize organizational performance, you won't spread development opportunities across the workforce like butter on bread. That is highly inequitable and flies in the face of good business principles. We make business investments based on our understanding of the return on that investment. When we provide differential treatment based on an understanding of the performance and potential of talent, we're providing the ultimate in fairness and doing right by the business.

≋ Generally, high potentials need much more attention in terms of assignments. They need to advance more quickly through a series of increasingly challenging positions. Their assignments should be closely matched to their development needs related to the development of key competencies and gaining perspective on the business.

Don't be afraid to differentiate. Differentiation is essential if you want to get the most out of your talent. Differentiation, if done well, is highly engaging. Setting clear expectations for your employees is important, and we started setting expectations before we made a hiring decision. In my monthly meeting with new employees, I addressed this issue. An abbreviated version goes something like this:

> *Good morning. It's a pleasure for me to meet each one of you and welcome you to our business. We do exciting work here, and each of you has an important role to play. Each of you will have an opportunity to do meaningful work and to build a successful and rewarding career. Each of you will have an opportunity to be challenged and learn and to develop your skills. And each of you will make a significant contribution to our success. We don't have non-contributors on our payroll.*

That said, we recognize that your contributions won't all be equal. We would not have hired you if we didn't believe you're motivated, but we recognize that some of you have an extra dose of motivation. Some of you have skills that others don't have. Each of you is an individual, and we recognize that. So, while everyone will have a great career and opportunities to learn and grow, some of you will be given challenges and opportunities that others don't receive. We are a meritocracy and recognize that you all provide value but you are all individuals. We will act accordingly.

As far as I know, no one ever complained about that message or mentioned it in an exit interview. We did our best to select people who would excel in our meritocracy and would find the message highly engaging rather than distasteful. So go ahead and differentiate. You'll do a better job of developing and engaging all employees.

Failure to differentiate will result in high potentials fleeing your organization in search of a meritocracy that recognizes their out-sized contribution and that provides them suitable career challenges. Failure to differentiate will result in disappointing many of those who stay behind and especially disappointing you because you'll be left with a mediocre workforce.

Recognition and rewards drive engagement

Here's a story that, for me, captures the essence of recognition as an engagement driver. Many years ago, when working as a maintenance supervisor, I attended a workshop on supervisory skills facilitated by an instructor from a local community college. She was a sharply dressed female who contrasted with the attendees, a bunch of gritty blue-collar guys. She was teaching us how to give effective feedback and reinforcement and asked if anyone ever had an experience of receiving reinforcement intended to be positive but that we didn't like.

An old buzzard in the last row chuckled and then regaled us with his tale. He told us that one day he walked into his small office just off the production floor to find a box on his desk. It was a watch, his 30-year service award. There was no note, nothing to indicate what it was for or even that it was for him. He knew what it was, though, because he'd recently had his 30-year anniversary and, after all, it was on his desk. The guy seemed to enjoy telling us how he marched with the watch to his boss's office and (these are his words) said, "Take the watch and the job and shove them both up your ass."

That's right. After 30 years with that organization, he quit on the spot. We all had a good laugh at the time, but I've reflected on that story many times since. I can only imagine that the guy was unhappy and waiting for any good excuse to quit. But still, there was a lesson in that story. From that day forward, I made sure to personalize reinforcement.

Here are my recommendations for leveraging this engagement driver:

ℹ Focus first on intangibles. When you consider the cost-benefit ratio, nothing beats simple verbal recognition for a job well done. If specific and authentic, it can be very powerful. And it costs you nothing. I'm also a fan of writing notes, but not at the expense of conversation. I used to have a stack of thank you cards in my desk and monthly reminder on my calendar that popped up to spur me to spend an hour writing notes to express appreciation to a handful of employees who'd really gone above and beyond that month. I kept my messages fairly short, but to the point, and made sure to address the specific contribution made and what it meant to the organization. I viewed those notes as an enhancement and semi-permanent reminder of a conversation, never as a substitute.

≋ Learn how to celebrate and publicly recognize outstanding performance. For some leaders this is natural and done well. Others are awkward or engage in grandstanding and really make a mess of things.

As with so many other leadership mistakes, ego is at the root. That's easy to see when a leader has a need to be the center of attention. But awkwardness caused by fear of making mistakes or embarrassing missteps is often, at its root, a desire to preserve some kind of image or popularity. That's ego. The offending leader is usually blind to his ego, but employees spot it a mile away. You can see it in exchanged glances and eye-rolling.

You'll much more effectively celebrate and provide public recognition if you leave your ego out of it. Make it about the team. Make it about the stellar performer who deserves your recognition. Don't assume you know how they want to celebrate or be recognized. Ask them. Customize your approach for them. It's all about them. It's never about you.

≈ Money is an engagement driver, and don't ever let anyone tell you it isn't. Some will tell you that pay is usually the lowest ranked item assessed in an engagement survey. They will further tell you that pay is not an effective motivator but can demotivate if people are underpaid. But for most people, it represents much more than food on the table and a roof overhead. It's status. It's a scorecard by which achievements are measured. It's what enables us to barter for that which makes us happy and fulfilled. It's an engagement driver.

To be an effective engagement driver, financial rewards should be commensurate with contribution, and I'm assuming I don't have to defend this statement. If you agree with that premise, the challenge is to accurately assess contribution so you can distribute money fairly.

Money (or any positive consequence) is a reward if it follows good performance. Money given before good performance is not a reward. In that case, it's bribery and often ineffective. When given as a reward, money drives engagement as long as it's dispensed fairly. If the distribution is perceived as unfair, however, it has a huge negative impact.

An employee can be perfectly happy with his salary, but watch out if he comes to believe that a peer is receiving, without justification, a higher financial reward. The sense of fairness can be hyper-sensitive. Violate it and you damage engagement.

The relationship with the boss drives engagement

I've saved the most powerful engagement driver for last. The relationship an employee has with their immediate boss is almost always the most important engagement driver. The boss relationship is an über-driver. The CEO can't create strategic alignment alone. The immediate boss either reinforces and teaches the business strategy or ignores it. Worst case, he can be a naysayer and rail against it. Any of these actions impacts strategic alignment for better or worse.

The immediate boss is a proxy for senior management. Employees often form an impression of senior management based on what they hear from their boss. The boss can promote confidence and trust in senior leadership or can tear it down. The immediate boss is the best position to understand development needs, to have career conversations, and to provide employees with opportunities to stretch and develop new skills and confidence. The immediate boss is the primary source of recognition and reward for employees. Related to rewards, the immediate boss can promote a sense of fairness or not.

For all these reasons, you need to focus on this boss relationship. Develop your people managers. Teach them how engagement works. All the engagement drivers mentioned are important. The boss relationship is essential.

Previously in the discussion about performance management, I described how we invested in preparing our people managers to have meaningful conversations and to provide performance and development coaching. I won't rehash those topics here, but I do want to reiterate that performance management is a primary vehicle for establishing a solid boss relationship and leveraging this engagement driver.

Engaging high potential talent

I've suggested that strategic alignment is, generally, a more important engagement driver for high potential employees. High potentials also tend to examine senior leaders more carefully and to care more deeply about the quality of your senior leadership team. High potentials are likely to be self-motivated learners and their development needs are primarily met by providing appropriately challenging assignments. I'll address this in the next couple of chapters in my journal.

High potentials place an especially high value on having influence. One of the best ways to provide them recognition is to ask for their opinions and respectfully listen. If you don't provide them opportunity to have a level of influence, they're likely to move to an employer that solicits and respects their opinions. Just remember that unless you're willing to engage in bribery, engagement is really the only way to retain your top talent.

Just imagine an entire workforce with the energy and sense of ownership demonstrated by young Miguel Angelo. That's what engagement will do for you.

Developing Talent

Day 5: January 3rd, Caribbean Sea

Last night I went to a magic show in the ship's theater with my wife and sister-in-law. For me, it was the first time in the theater, but the ladies had seen *Hairspray* the previous evening and insisted that I go to a show with them. I was glad it was a magic show. I don't mind a good staged drama or comedy, but musicals always put me to sleep.

The place was crowded, but we got there early and had seats in the front row. The magician was talented, and the audience was into it, duly impressed with the illusions and showmanship. At one point he asked for a volunteer, scanned the front row, and selected Carol, my sister-in-law.

This is where the show got interesting. If I hadn't personally known Carol and that she was not his shill, I would never have believed that what happened next was not an elaborately scripted comedy routine.

The comedy started when the magician asked Carol to select one of three large vases sitting on a table on the stage. Carol was all atwitter, very nervous at being on stage in front of hundreds of people. In her nervousness, she was a little too enthusiastic when pointing to her preferred vase. Her hand made contact and knocked it over.

It was filled with liquid that appeared to be water, but whatever it was, it must have had a low coefficient of friction. Carol lunged to try to catch the vase, lost her balance, and fell on the table. The whole works collapsed,

Carol on top. The magician rushed to help her up, but the floor was now wet and slippery, and his feet went out from under him.

The resulting pratfall was spectacular. His feet arched toward the ceiling lights and his head cracked on the stage. The audience gawked in stunned silence for just the briefest moment while they were trying to figure out if this was all planned, but the silence was for only a split second. Then the entire auditorium erupted, half in raucous laughter and the other half in groans of concern.

A couple of stagehands rushed in from the wings to help Carol up, and as she raised her hindquarters, hands still on the floor, the poor old gal broke wind. It wasn't a squeak, and the stage was miked. Carol unleashed a resounding toot that reached the last row of the auditorium. Of course, this ill-timed flatulence ignited a fit of laughter that raised the roof.

The whole spectacle was truly amazing, but on reflection, what happened next was no less so. While the stagehands were helping Carol recover, arms wrapping around her and whispering in her ear, the emcee stepped on stage and dramatically described how new cast members were very carefully selected and then announced that Carol had just passed her audition.

The stagehands had somehow prevented Carol from fleeing the stage in humiliation. They must have been whispering instructions while the announcement was made because, as soon as the emcee finished, she turned around to face the audience. With a thin smile tentatively emerging on her beet-red face, Carol courageously stepped forward, hand-in-hand with the stagehands, and took a deep bow to a standing ovation.

The magician had managed to shake off the blow to his head and shakily get to his feet. He embraced Carol in a big hug and then joined in the bows as the curtains closed. Immediately a guitar-playing singer entered, stage right, sat a stool in front of the curtain, and said that while the stage was being set for the "second act," he'd take a few requests. This entire disastrous episode had the appearance of being meticulously planned and rehearsed.

How in the world did those cast members know how to deal with such a fiasco? How did the cruise line prepare employees to deal with such chaos? I'm sure I don't have all the answers, but I can share my insights into developing talent and the practices that worked for my company. And perhaps I have more insight in this area than some other CEOs.

As CEO, I was much more involved in the development of our talent than is typical. Most executives, I think, see development as a necessary cost of doing business. As much as you might hate to, you've got to pay some taxes. You've got to pay some lawyers. And you've got to spend some money on training. Even when they genuinely and passionately believe in the importance of development, most CEOs aren't deeply engaged in it. There are always so many other priorities, always bigger fish. Most CEOs don't actively get involved in development. I did.

It's always been fascinating for me to study how people learn, and I love to teach. But engaging in talent development was more than self-gratification. My business success was driven by the capabilities of my people. We were constantly pushing the envelope through innovation. Jobs were constantly changing. Technology was constantly changing. My people needed to constantly change too. I needed my managers to make development a priority. If

I gave more than lip service, so would they. If I got really engaged in development, so would they. And if I became a role model for managing the quality and impact of development, so would they.

Training vs. development

Enhancing employee capabilities, for me, consists of two related activities that vary in terms of timeframe, focus, and methods. I'll use the term *training* to refer to activities that primarily focus on technical competencies, impact current and near-term performance, and consist of managed events that adhere to particular design specifications. I'll use the term *development* to refer to activities that mainly focus on broader leadership competencies, have a long-term impact, and are usually part of a messy process that's tangled up with (and sometimes indistinguishable from) the job itself.

Training and development are not distinct or mutually exclusive. Both build capabilities and cause learning to occur. Both create a fundamental change in the learner. And both lead to enhanced performance and contribution to the organization. Much of what I share about training applies to development, and vice versa. Based on my deep involvement in the development of my workforce, here are my recommendations:

First, understand what drives performance

My view of performance is pretty simple, and when an employee isn't performing as desired, I chalk it up to one of three root causes. The first is a knowing problem: the employee doesn't know what to do or doesn't know how to do it. The second root cause is a wanting problem: the employee doesn't want to do it. And the third root cause is an environmental problem: something in the environment is hindering the employee from performing. Three root causes. Simple.

Nine times out of ten, the root cause is the environment. And who controls the environment? Managers do. Managers are in charge of the environment. Managers provide direction, set the pace, provide the tools for the job, remove obstacles that aren't in the employee's control, reinforce good performance, and correct substandard performance. If an employee isn't performing as expected, look first to make sure hindrances are removed from the environment.

When there's a motivation issue, it's often just a symptom of the true root cause, the environment. Always look to the environment first when you have an underperforming employee. You hire people you believe to be competent and motivated. They start the job with a good attitude, wanting to succeed and expecting to succeed.

In the real world, there aren't too many George Costanzas who show up the first day on the job as if in a Seinfeld episode looking to hide in an office with the Penske file or nap under a desk. If an employee starts the first day motivated and six months or six years later has an attitude problem, the environment is the most likely cause. In other words, the manager hasn't taken care of the environment. The manager hasn't done his job.

Performance problems resulting from a lack of knowledge and skills occur when the employee encounters something new—a new job, a new process, a new technology, even a new customer—anything new. Be sure you understand the need before you identify a cure. Be sure to understand the root cause of performance problems so you don't put time and energy into ineffective solutions.

Understand the nature and intent of training

When you have a problem caused by a lack of knowledge and skills, you can choose to change the job or to change the person. Training changes the person because it creates learning, an internal change in the learner. To learn is to acquire the ability to do something new. You can't separate learning from behavior—you must be able to do something to prove you've learned something. You're a different person after learning because you've internalized an ability that you didn't have before you learned it.

Training is an event, an experience designed to cause learning. As an event, training has a beginning and an end and must include at least three components:

1. Content (concepts, principles, procedures, rules, etc.) related to what's being learned

2. Opportunities to practice the behavior that demonstrates learning

3. Evaluation and feedback on the practiced behavior

During the training experience, a trainer or facilitator controls instructional variables, manipulates them to optimize the learning experience. Examples are the organization of content, type of practice activities, media used, layout of the training space, pacing used to present content, etc.

Facilitator-led training obviously relies to some degree on the skill of the facilitator. Good facilitators are able to adapt the presentation of content and practice activities to the audience to better engage and impact learners. But good facilitators can't completely compensate for bad design. Some training programs are designed to be navigated independently at a pace chosen by the learner. Some training programs are designed so that much of the meaning is constructed by the learner rather than dictated by someone else. In these types of programs especially, training effectiveness demands a skilled designer. Never underestimate the importance of design for all training programs.

Our previous discussion of engagement certainly applies to training effectiveness. Engagement is about ownership, about taking responsibility. Without the engagement of learners and their active participation, your training programs will suck. The most effective programs are those in which every party is totally engaged and responsible. The learner assumes responsibility for her success. The facilitator feels responsible for her success. And so does the designer. But let's not forget the manager.

Remember that the boss relationship is generally the most powerful engagement driver. That applies in training situations too. Effective training requires managers who reinforce the new skills and behaviors learned during training. If managers fail to reinforce learned behaviors and to provide opportunities for those behaviors to be practiced, you will waste time, money, and energy by providing training.

101

Carefully consider the nature of the jobs and tasks

The complexity of your jobs can work to your advantage. This is an intuitive conclusion if you have a craft-oriented business, but it can apply to many businesses. Complexity presents a barrier to entry for competitors and may represent a competitive advantage if that complexity is best addressed by employees' knowledge and skill rather than through job reengineering. Paradoxically, you must recognize that needless job complexity works against you and negatively impacts efficiency and quality and adds friction to your processes.

It may be obvious that you'll benefit by continuously finding new ways to simplify jobs and to build intelligence into jobs. It may be less obvious that if jobs are simplified and the same workforce does those simpler jobs, you're probably going to end up with major employee engagement problems.

When you decrease the job intelligence required for a job, look for opportunities to leverage the creativity and intellectual horsepower of your workforce in other ways. Look for opportunities to enrich the job by expanding the scope and asking them to shoulder more responsibilities. Look for opportunities to more fully engage your employees' brains to innovate, to create the new and different.

Doing this with forethought and intention is a way to build organizational capabilities that provide a strategic advantage. Failing to do this puts talent at risk, makes you a less formidable competitor, and opens the door for your competition to rapidly catch up. If you don't thoroughly understand this issue and its implications, you don't fully understand your business.

Always consider the alternatives to training

When some elements of a job change, you may find that there are performance problems caused by not knowing what to do or how to do it. But let's face it, there's really no excuse for an employee not knowing *what* to do. There's no excuse for a manager not setting clear expectations. When an employee doesn't know what to do, you tell them. Duh. If expectations aren't clear, you have a management problem. Fix it.

When an employee doesn't know *how* to do something, it's more complicated. You need to decide to what extent you'll change the employee by training to instill new knowledge and skills and to what extent you'll reengineer the job so it requires less of the employee.

As indicated above, you can build in job intelligence so less skill is required. This is normally done through automating manual processes, building in computing power, and/or addressing the human factors engineering through better design of controls, displays, tools, workstation, job aids, etc. This is fascinating stuff, one of my passions, but my intent here is to just provide some food for thought related to job design. To dig deeper, I recommend you start with Donald Norman's books on design.

Think through all the consequences before investing in training employees. Be smart about it. Consider all your alternatives. Training is generally overused because it's inappropriately identified as a solution to a performance problem. Most performance problems are not caused by a lack of knowledge and skills. Even when you've done a good job of diagnosing the performance issues, you should consider other alternatives to training because of four fundamental problems:

1. Training is expensive when compared to many other potential solutions, such as job aids.

2. There are always scheduling difficulties. You think you're getting around that by providing asynchronous programs that allow for independent study and providing flexibility with web-based instruction. You're mistaken if you think these totally solve scheduling problems for your employees. They have competing priorities, and it seems there's never enough time.

3. The knowledge and skills learned in training are temporary. If employees aren't given adequate opportunity to practice and receive feedback and reinforcement after the training event, they will almost surely lose what they learned.

4. Training is transient, that is, it moves with the learner. Your training investment changes the learner and travels with the learner. This point deserves a note of caution.

Yes, training moves with the learner. Yes, it's possible that you'll invest in training an employee only to have them leave and maybe even join a competitor. But never use this as an excuse to not train an employee. It's far better to have a trained employee leave than to have an incompetent employee stay.

Aggressively implement job aids

Just as a tool leverages your physical capabilities, a job aid leverages your mental capabilities. You should identify a handful of employees in your organization representing a variety of functions and challenge them to develop some expertise in analyzing jobs and developing job aids. Examples include apps of all sorts—and not just computer-based apps. Job aids include checklists, decision aids, calculators, algorithms, flow charts, etc.

Job aids make us smarter. They store job intelligence outside of the learner and serve as a great way to document expertise and reduce the need for training. Apply job aids as a way to simplify complex jobs and ensure that critical tasks are done correctly.

I'm surrounded by job aids on the cruise ship: maps, schedules, instructions, checklists, and a huge variety of apps I can access through my TV and phone to assist me if I want to plan a shore excursion, order a meal, or even to buy jewelry or purchase new eyeglasses. It feels like I'm on a floating mall. But the point is that job aids are everywhere, and most everyone takes them for granted. Don't.

Don't leave app development to pimpled teenagers working in their parents' basement. You can use apps—all sorts of job aids—to support your business. Although they may appear simple, there's a science and discipline to developing effective job aids. As you consider your approach to training, also consider job aids.

Job aids are typically unnecessary for tasks that are done frequently as a routine. Routine tasks are naturally learned and reinforced with the frequent doing.

There are exceptions when the consequences of error are extreme. It's OK for your pilot to use a checklist prior to takeoff or your nurse to use a pre-op checklist before you undergo surgery. Even if pilots and nurses have the procedures memorized, you can't afford mistakes in the air or the operating room.

However, job aids are not appropriate to support tasks that are performed in urgent circumstances. When a jet engine sucks in a large bird and you only have a couple of minutes to put the plane down on the Hudson River, you don't want your pilot reaching for a job aid.

And some task requirements are too unpredictable to be amenable to a job aid. There's no checklist to follow when a flatulent guest wreaks havoc on the stage during a magic show.

There are times we want to over-train employees to deal with urgent situations. If I ask you "what does 7 times 8 equal?" you should respond immediately with the correct answer: 56. If you can't do that without thinking about it, you may be cursing your third grade teacher to this day. Some things should be over-learned just like you (hopefully) over-learned your multiplication tables.

Smart training is fiscally responsible

In addition to the considerations discussed above, it should go without saying that it's important to apply financial savvy and discipline to training. I found this more difficult than expected. Have you ever had what seemed like a great idea but in hindsight wondered how you could have conceived of something so dopey? I've had many such ideas, and at least one of them was related to training.

Early on, in my zeal to build skills in my workforce, I suggested to my HR manager that we implement a policy to ensure that all of our employees receive a minimum of 80 hours of training per year. Isabel was aghast and took me to task, told me that it wasn't at all like me to implement such a silly policy.

I remember being totally surprised and even a little wounded by her reaction. That she called the policy silly was twisting the knife in the wound. After all, we both agreed that our business would only succeed on the skills of our workforce. We both were training aficionados. What could be wrong with establishing a minimum to ensure that no one would be neglected and fail to receive training opportunities that could meaningfully enhance their contribution? How could she oppose such a great idea?

Isabel gave a stinging response, but her use of the word "we" took the edge off. "Do we really want to implement rules and manage training through compliance? Compliance and rules have their place. There are some rules we have to follow to make sure we work safely. There are laws and regulations we have to follow. But we've worked hard to remove unnecessary rules because they create bureaucracy and friction in our work. We want our people to desire to learn. We don't want to force them. We want them to choose. Our people would view this decision as something they need to do to be in compliance. It would represent a step backward for our culture."

She continued, "But the main reason we don't want to do this is that it's not good business. We work really hard to make smart decisions with our capital, and training costs a lot of money. We agree that training is valuable when focused on the right kind of performance problems, but some of our folks might not need 80 hours every year.

Others might need considerably more in a given year. We invest our capital where it's needed, where it provides the best return. We don't spread it around like peanut butter."

I saw her point. Like I said, it was kind of a dopey idea.

We learned to invest intelligently in targeted training. Almost all of the programs I'd classify as training (event-based) were focused on building functional and technical competencies. We didn't have a huge training staff but did have several experts in instructional design who also had considerable knowledge of business and our particular technologies. Without that knowledge, I don't believe they would have been effective. Our technical training programs were facilitated almost exclusively by our own subject matter experts, and our designers had to be able to communicate with these people and speak in their language. More on this later.

We also provided training (event-based) programs that addressed some leadership competencies such as conflict management, and I earlier described some training conducted in support of performance management that included leadership competency development. For the most part, though, we approached the development of leadership competencies (e.g., negotiating, delegating, innovating, etc.) differently than we did the development of technical competencies (e.g., materials testing, tooling design, programming, etc.).

It takes more than training

Let's shift our focus to development, which, like training, results in the ability to do something new, but development is not an event. Development is a less structured experience and largely, sometimes entirely, under the control of the learner. Both result in learning. Both must have objectives—the targeted new behaviors that will result. Both must include opportunities for practice, opportunities to try—and potentially fail—to reach the objective. And both must include some kind of feedback so the learner can make adjustments during subsequent practice. Eventually the behavior is learned. It is internalized and repeatable.

In a training event, the content, practice, and assessment are planned. They're designed. They're handed to the learner on a silver platter. Outside of a training event, development is different. There is less planning. The learner usually must be on the lookout for opportunities to practice and perhaps fail. Assessment and feedback isn't always built-in like it is in a training event, so the learner must be engaged and sensitive to feedback. They must proactively solicit feedback.

What we do in development is to provide goal focus and accelerate what normally happens in life. Life can be defined as one long series of problems. The normal maturation process is to acquire new skills—to develop—as you try to solve life's problems. You want to walk so you try. You fall down a lot at first, but eventually, after trial and error, you learn. In the same way you learn to talk. You learn to ride a bike. You learn to drive.

And, if you're a good student in life, you learn to control your temper when some dumbass in the left lane is slowing you down. You learn these things as a normal outcome of maturing. To live is to learn to solve life's problems. This can be a slow process. I can personally attest to the fact that some people never do learn to control their temper when the fast lane is blocked.

Accelerating development

In business, we need people who can inspire and engage others, who can manage innovation, who can effectively lead change. We don't have the luxury of letting people learn these things by accident or as part of their normal maturation process. But for the most part, these skill sets are not learned in an event. Sure, you can learn some principles and develop a vocabulary in a training program. But we're talking about big, hairy, complex skill sets that are too big to fit entirely within a training program. Big, hairy, complex skill sets are learned through life experience.

To develop these types of complex skill sets, we accelerate the learning process by doing the following:

- *Provide focus.* We need to point our employees in the right direction. I'm all for employees directing their own development, but we can't leave it all up to them. Most of us pursue what we like, what's comfortable. We usually like what we do reasonably well. We usually dislike what's outside of our comfort zone, but that's where learning occurs.

  We have a responsibility to nudge people in the direction of what's important for the business and for their career success, especially when those things lie outside of the employee's comfort zone. Help your employees focus on what's important, not on what's most comfortable.

- *Set expectations.* Let employees know what skill sets are most critical for the success of the business. Help them understand that, as in life, most learning occurs when we're in challenging situations. Let them know how successful careers are built. Explain that sometimes it's the jobs that we most hate that are the very ones to catapult our career.

Let them know that if they find themselves in a job that's unlike anything they've ever done before, and it's a job they detest, and it's also a job that has severe consequences for screwing up, they should count themselves fortunate. They're likely to look back on the job and realize it was a turning point, the time in which they learned and grew more than at any other point in their career.

≈ *Create opportunities.* We learn by doing jobs. Assigning employees to jobs in which they will learn key competencies and gain needed perspectives on the business is the single most powerful way we can develop employees. It's not possible, though, to meet all development needs with full-time jobs. We don't have enough key developmental jobs in the organization. And managing a continual mass movement of the workforce through jobs is untenable.

We have to look beyond full-time jobs to projects, task forces, and other extracurricular and part-time assignments that stretch employees beyond their current job without requiring them to leave that job. Your managers need to learn to spot those opportunities where they do exist and create legitimate opportunities where they don't exist. They need to learn to match employee needs with the skills and perspectives taught by those opportunities. They need to be highly skilled at delegation, which, in this case, is the primary vehicle for development.

≋ *Assess and reinforce.* If you want to accelerate development, you need to be timely with feedback so employees can more frequently adjust and practice new behaviors. In a training event, there is practice, assessment, and feedback built into the design. Without the structure of a training event, your managers need to proactively monitor progress toward development goals, provide feedback, and reinforce advancement. They should recognize efforts made in the face of challenges.

It's almost impossible to overemphasize the importance of feedback and reinforcement. It should be the centerpiece of many meaningful conversations between your managers and employees.

≋ *Make learning connections.* Have meaningful conversations with the employee about lessons learned. Ask them how they're applying previous learning to their new challenges. Encourage them to reflect. Ask them to verbalize what they've learned. Point out the impact of their behaviors on their team and the organization. Point out the implications for what they're learning. By doing this we're helping them to learn to practice conscious awareness of their capability and confidence level. You're helping them develop emotional intelligence. Self-awareness, the ability to accurately self-monitor, is a key component of emotional intelligence and an enabler of self-directed learning.

≋ *Make network and coaching connections.* Connect employees to others who are on similar developmental paths. Connect them to those who have previously navigated similar learning experiences. If you want to learn something, teach it to others. If you want to master a competency, it's helpful to verbalize the lessons you've learned. There's no better way to do this than by coaching others. Facilitate those relationships.

Learning organizations are those in which nearly everyone is a coach to someone else. Often the coach gains more from the coaching than the learner, but the truth is that a culture of coaching elevates learning across the organization. You and your managers can create such a culture.

≋ *Develop the right leadership competencies.*
A competency is a skill that we can observe and measure and contributes to our on-the-job success. I've previously described two types of competencies. Technical competencies are needed to be successful in specific roles. When I was a working as a welder, I could weld an open-root pipe joint in the 6G position using an E6010 electrode. Perfect keyhole. Slick as a brick. Chances are, you don't need that skill to be successful, but I did.

Leadership competencies apply, at least to some extent, to nearly all roles. Unless you're a lighthouse keeper, you probably need some degree of skill in managing conflict to succeed. Virtually everyone benefits from demonstrating interpersonal skills. And who doesn't need skill in listening? Competencies are important because they give us a language to describe how work gets done. Competencies give us a vocabulary for coaching. They focus our development.

All of us are a walking bundle of competencies, and our relative strengths and weaknesses give us a leadership texture. The question is, do we have the right texture? Functional-technical competencies clearly change as the nature of jobs change. But so does the importance of various leadership competencies change as your career progresses. Focus your development efforts on matching your leadership texture to the needs of your current and future roles.

There's a lot of confusion about which competencies should be developed. Let's cut through the crap. There are three primary considerations for deciding what should be in your development plan.

1. First, consider what's important. What competencies are critical to your success in your current role? In your next role? If you're a project manager, you better have planning, process management, and organizing skills at the forefront of your competency texture. If you're aspiring to the role of CEO, you better have skills in dealing with ambiguity, envisioning the future and creating strategy, and leading senior teams. And there are other skills, of course, that are essential for success as a project manager or as a CEO. Know the critical skills that apply to you and your employees.

2. Second, consider your strengths and weaknesses. And don't trust your own evaluation. Ask for feedback from those you trust and know you well. Get 360 feedback. Get other assessments of personality and skills and carefully consider the results. Drop all your defensiveness and consider that almost no one fully comprehends

her own leadership texture, especially her weaknesses.

3. Finally, consider the difficulty of developing key skills. Some competencies are much more difficult to develop than others. They take more time. More effort. More practice. Learning to listen well and to manage your time isn't so tough. Learning to craft an effective strategy will probably take you a number of years.

Development is hard work

If a competency is mission-critical for your current or next role and you're not skilled, develop that competency aggressively. If you're serious about this, you don't have time to be hanging out at the pool or lying about on a cruise ship. Competency development is hard work. Some competencies are a real bitch, and those tend to be the ones that are most important.

Focus on your relative weaknesses. Your strengths are in your comfort zone and will mostly take care of themselves. My Grandma use to chide me when I was sweeping the kitchen, "Get the corners good, Jack. The rest takes care of itself." You've got weaknesses hiding in the corners, and some of them will bite you on the ass if you don't deal with them. Your weaknesses can create a career ceiling for you. They can drive your career off a cliff.

People love to work on their strengths. Why not? If we're pretty good at something, we like it. It's comfortable to work on our strengths. It's uncomfortable to work on our weaknesses. Uncomfortable but essential.

This guideline may be modified for high potential specialists, those who are on a technical career path. Deep experts have a passion for their discipline and thousands of hours of focused practice invested in developing their expertise. Their expertise is their strength, and as long as they intend to continue contributing as a deep expert, they should continue to develop that strength. They cannot, however, ignore their weaknesses.

We created programs to accelerate development and customized them for different talent pools. These programs integrated assessment and coaching to help make learning connections and raise self-awareness. They afforded a networking opportunity to link learners facing similar challenges. We set expectations about how careers are built and helped focus our employees on the right competencies for development. We utilized learning projects to give meaningful assignments that had both organizational and developmental benefits.

One of the most important things we did in these programs, I think, was to institutionalize the sharing of our experiences and creating scenarios that built upon those experiences. Our high potential generalists played out scenarios related to the competitive landscape, threats to our strategy, changes to our value chain, etc. Our high potential specialists played out scenarios related to technology. They spent a lot of time deconstructing technical problems and creating scenarios involving previously unimagined problems. These practices became habits that gave us organizational agility and innovation capability.

I cannot imagine that the crew members who responded so splendidly to the on-stage crisis last night had been able to foresee and practice that exact scenario. I can, however, imagine that a network of stagehands shared stories of crises they'd encountered. Passengers who'd become sick or drunk or violent. Equipment malfunctions. Wardrobe malfunctions. Perhaps they actively shared experiences and spent time envisioning and predicting the unpredictable. Almost assuredly they spent time mentally rehearsing responses to various emergencies that couldn't be easily practiced in a traditional training experience.

One thing is certain, what happened last night was a real-life experience that provided them valuable lessons that will shape their future behaviors and likely be shared with many others. That's development.

Deploying Talent

Day 6: January 4th, Caribbean Sea

My sister-in-law's performance in the magic show has earned her celebrity status. People keep stopping her to tell her how funny she is, and several have asked her to autograph their daily activities program. Carol finds the notoriety invigorating, but my wife, not so much. She would never admit to it, but I think Betsy's actually a little jealous of her sister.

Personally, I don't think I'm much given to jealousy. I guess I might allow a little envy for the guys listed in Boone & Crockett with whitetail records, but I can't for the life of me imagine being jealous of the attention received for tripping onstage and cutting one loose in front of a large audience.

Last night we were invited to dine with the magician, emcee, and the two employees who helped Carol onstage. I think the idea was to provide some recognition for the quick-thinking stage hands but also to make sure that Carol was taking things well and not feeling litigious. They needn't worry. She's already making plans for her next cruise.

The magician's stage moniker, Devon Devitri, has a nice ring to it. When I pressed him, he admitted he changed his name from Boyd Smolanski when he left Sheboygan for Vegas to work on his magic act. He didn't have to explain further. I figured that a kid from Sheboygan with a name like Boyd couldn't be all bad, but I kept a close eye on him during dinner nonetheless. I suspected he might be tempted to amuse us with some magic, maybe turn my rib eye into a rutabaga. But Boyd was pretty quiet, and the dinner was illusion-free.

Cedric, the emcee, however, was quite chatty. He proudly handed me his business card, which gave his title as Theater Manager, and I asked him to tell us about his career. He gladly obliged: a black kid from the projects in Baltimore, who joined the Navy after high school and worked as a cook, left the service and spent two years studying business at the University of Maryland but had to drop out when his mom got sick. Cedric joined the cruise line five years ago and had several jobs in the first three years: tended bar, dealt blackjack in the casino, and worked as a supervisor in housekeeping. Then, two years ago, his manager nominated him for the company's hotel management program.

Cedric told us about the experience of going through a company-sponsored leadership assessment center, meeting with a coach for feedback, and a variety of development experiences he'd already received. He was excited about his career prospects and said he believed his company is really actively interested in his career and is pushing him hard with stretch assignments.

As evidence, Cedric said that six months ago his boss had a conversation with him and told him about the opportunity to take on the role of theater manager. It was explained that this role would give him an opportunity to polish his self-presentation and develop speaking skills. Specifically, he was told he needed to gain self-confidence and to speak more clearly and professionally. His sloppy use of English and lack of professional image was going to hold him back, and his boss didn't hesitate to tell him so.

Cedric considered the job offer to be both exciting and terrifying. He said he nearly wet himself the first few times he had to get on stage to introduce a show, but now he loved it and could feel his confidence growing daily.

His degree of transformation can only be imagined, but I can attest that last night Cedric was articulate and professional. And justifiably proud. The stagehands at the table were hanging on his words, probably wondering if they would receive the same opportunity as their boss had been given. Cedric, by telling his story, was opening their eyes to possibilities, and the hotel management program was looking good.

There's not much more I can tell you about Cedric's career or how he's viewed by his organization, but my sense is that he was identified as an emerging high potential and is being groomed for bigger and better things as part of a rigorous succession planning process.

Succession planning vs. replacement planning

Succession is my topic of the day, but I've headed this journal chapter as "deploying talent" rather than succession planning because there's a lot of confusion about this topic. Most organizations claim to do succession planning but really don't. They do replacement planning yet believe they're doing succession planning. Jack gets hit by a bus. Who's in line to fill Jack's shoes? That's not succession planning. Replacement planning is not succession planning.

Succession planning is the process of systematically managing the deployment of key talent into suitable jobs to accomplish two objectives: 1) meet the current operating needs of the business, and 2) develop a robust talent pipeline to ensure there are ready candidates to move into key positions in the future.

These two objectives are at odds. If you want to be sure that jobs are done right, you'll select proven talent, people who've demonstrated they can do the job. On the other hand, if you're trying to develop talent so they're ready for more responsible positions, you're going to put them into jobs in which they're going to be stretched and learn and grow. Remember, these two important principles: 1) we learn most of what we need for success by doing jobs, and 2) we don't learn anything unless we have an opportunity to fail.

You see the dilemma? If you deploy people into jobs in which they lack capability, they put the business at risk. And if you deploy people into jobs for which they're already fully capable, they don't have room to develop.

Finding your way through this paradox is the crux of succession planning. We found this process challenging but extremely valuable. Our succession practices helped us engage, develop, and retain our top talent. We created a strong leadership bench. And we found our talent reviews to be the single most effective way to raise the level of talent management sophistication in our management ranks.

We learned important lessons, and I'll share some of what worked for us in each of these succession planning phases:

1. *Workforce Planning:* Forecasting future talent needs and developing a build-versus-buy strategy

2. *Key Position Analysis:* Identifying seminal jobs, the royalty positions at the end of the talent pipelines

3. *Talent Reviews:* Thoroughly understanding and rigorously differentiating the current inventory of talent

4. *Deployment and Development:* Managing the execution of the succession plan

Workforce planning

Our HR team did the lion's share of the work to prepare our workforce plan by analyzing data, anticipating changes in our need for key competencies required to execute the business strategy, forecasting talent gaps by function and business unit, and using projections to shape our build-versus-buy strategy for talent.

The output of our annual strategic planning process was the source of the most important data considered in crafting our workforce plan. In fact, workforce planning was the primary bridge between our business strategy and our talent management strategy. Here are the primary steps we followed:

1. Summarize current workforce demographic data and skills inventory

2. Review available economic and labor market trends and projections

3. Analyze the company's strategic business plan with regard to changing organizational

capabilities and core competencies required to achieve the plan

4. Taking all the above into account, project growth rates, turnover, and resulting gaps in headcount and key competencies for key functions and by business unit

5. Engage in scenario planning to test the plan, identify possible but low-probability situations, and create contingency plans

6. Document recommendations for our recruiting tactics for the coming business cycle, prepare budgets for compensation, benefits, and training, and create an executive summary

My role in all of this was to provide input when asked during creation of the plan and then to review the completed plan in detail with my senior leadership team. We discussed the implications, challenged the assumptions and conclusions, debated the recommendations, and often suggested revisions.

Key position analysis

I've frequently heard the term "talent pipeline" glibly tossed about without much thought to a shared definition. To my way of thinking, a talent pipeline is a broad career pathway, often with alternate routes, that leads to a key position in the organization. The pathway is sprinkled with way stations, jobs mostly, that provide development experiences for employees as they navigate their career. As the final destination nears, the pathway narrows, and the vast majority of travelers stop at a way station short of the final destination. Many may be on the path, but very few employees actually ascend to what I call a royalty position, the terminal position for a talent pipeline.

One of the most common misconceptions is that an organization has but one talent pipeline. We managed several talent pipelines, career paths that prepared talent capable of serving in our royalty positions. The skill sets and perspectives for the royalty positions were different and, of necessity, required different development way stations. The career pathways for each diverged in order to provide the right experiences.

We defined royalty positions as those select few positions in the organization that are both very difficult to do and that have very high strategic value because they directly drive the unique value proposition of the firm. Identifying royalty positions is not difficult but is fraught with political sensitivities.

Early on we tried doing this with a team comprised of managers from different functions. Big surprise, it seemed that everyone argued that his job should be considered a royalty position. After a few difficult meetings, I assigned the task of classifying positions to Isabel and then reviewed her analysis. We reviewed our position analysis annually and revised as required.

Determining the difficulty of a position isn't too difficult. Actually, you've pretty much done this when you assess a job for compensable factors. We generally pay more for jobs that are more difficult and more complex. In addition to considering the compensation for the position, you can ask yourself how difficult it is to find people who can do the job and consider what special skills and experiences are required.

In addition to difficulty, you need to also evaluate jobs in terms of strategic contribution to the organization. To do this, you need to objectively—stress on objectively—consider how essential the job is in terms of driving the unique value proposition and providing mission-critical contributions to delivering the strategy. If a job can conceivably be done by a contractor, even if it's extremely complex, it's not likely a driver of your value proposition.

You can map key jobs on a two-dimensional grid with one axis representing difficulty and the other representing strategic value. If you go through this process, you will have a valuable map of key jobs in your firm that can provide guidance when developing and deploying talent. To illustrate its applications, here's a simplified map with only a few jobs from our business placed on the grid.

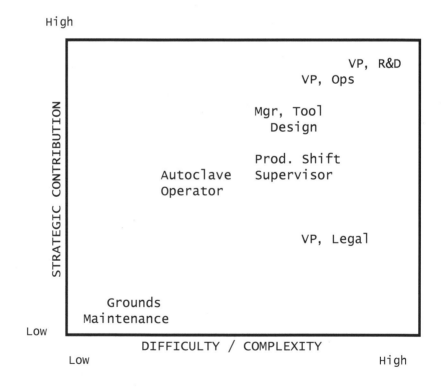

Mapping jobs in this way is useful for identifying the royalty positions, the ones in the extreme upper right corner. You could stop there, but I think there is value in spending time to flesh out the map with all positions that are highly compensated or which have many incumbents. The mapping might come in handy as an input to decisions about restructuring, outsourcing, etc.

You'll probably find that many of your jobs cluster in the middle and, frankly, aren't quite as interesting as the jobs that map out toward the corners. Jobs in the lower left-hand corner are those that are low in complexity and of relatively low strategic value to the firm. These are the jobs that may be candidates for outsourcing if you're so inclined. We did periodically analyze these positions to determine if it made sense to outsource. As examples, we outsourced cafeteria services and grounds maintenance but decided against outsourcing facilities maintenance and security.

Jobs in the lower right-hand corner can be a distraction. These jobs are high in difficulty and complexity but relatively low in strategic contribution. People in these jobs tend to have high expectations for development and career support, and understandably so. They are typically highly compensated and work in professions that require lots of education and may have certification or licensing requirements.

Often these lower right-hand positions are from your enabling functions such as finance, legal, IT, and HR. If you're brutally honest and objective, you'll admit that, for most organizations, these positions are enablers of the strategy but not the drivers of your strategy.

Our most senior finance, legal, and IT people were strategic thinkers and contributed to creating and executing our strategy. But our customers would never say they bought from our firm because of finance or legal or IT capabilities. Please don't misunderstand. We did build capabilities in our enabling functions and aimed to promote from within, but they didn't merit the same level of consideration as royalty positions.

The positions that map into the upper left-hand corner are troublesome and worthy of your attention. If you have positions that are truly mission-critical to your strategy but that are not difficult or complex, you should ask yourself if your strategy is defensible or can be easily replicated by your competition. If easily replicated, any competitive advantages these positions contribute are probably short-lived. Take some time to reflect on this and how it relates to the previous discussion about the nature of jobs and tasks.

The positions in the upper right-hand corner are those upon which your organization rises or falls. These are the royalty positions. They should be the focus of your succession planning. You should be aggressively developing bench strength for these positions and promoting from within to fill them.

You can be transparent about the value of these positions. Employees are bright enough to know that not all jobs are created equal. Why make it a secret that these jobs are the primary drivers of your value proposition?

Talent reviews

At the heart of succession planning is the talent review, a rigorous discussion between peers about the talent for which they're responsible. Talent reviews help us comprehend our inventory of talent, differentiate talent in multiple dimensions, and make decisions related to deployment and development. And to reinforce a point I've made previously, remember that you can't really separate deployment from development.

If you're in an organization of any size, it's likely to be impractical and unnecessary to invest enough in talent reviews to have peer discussions of all talent. In my firm, we started one level up from the supervisor level and ran talent reviews in two tracks—one track for functional-technical talent and another track for generalists. Management teams would convene—a group of peers and their boss—and review the talent one level below and also include selected early-career employees who were lower in position level but identified as emerging talent. The reviews cascaded up and culminated with a two-day annual talent review in which the senior team and I would review as many as 70 senior managers and high potential employees.

Our formal, comprehensive talent reviews were conducted annually, but we also had frequent talent discussions in my weekly management team meeting and we formally devoted at least 30 minutes to talent every month in our operations meeting. We paid as much attention to talent in our management meetings as we did to finance, sales, and operations.

In our talent reviews, we differentiated talent on three dimensions, the three Ps: Performance, Path, and Potential.

Assessing performance

This shouldn't be difficult to assess. For most managers, it is. In addition to the bias and other problems that afflict so many managers, I've seen how difficult it is to objectively and realistically assess the total contribution of an individual over time. It's pretty easy to consider only the current business cycle and to simply ask, "Did they make their numbers?"

In our talent reviews, I asked that we consider a rolling three-year average of performance and take into account effort and context in addition to looking at whether or not they made their numbers. There are situations in which an individual fails to meet all their objectives because of unpredictable conditions, yet they made a supreme effort and accomplished more than others could have in the same situation.

I am generally a tough evaluator, and with the benefit of hindsight, it's easy to be a hard-ass. It's more difficult but more accurate if you can maintain rigor while objectively stepping back from the situation and considering the whole picture—the value of what the employee delivered, the effort required to achieve the results, and the difficulty posed by environment. This should be the nature of the performance conversations in talent reviews.

Identifying career path

Many, if not most, of your employees were hired because they had a particular set of skills. They started with your organization as a specialist of some kind—an accountant, a programmer, a machinist. And many, if not most, of your employees will change specializations during their career, perhaps several times. Typical employees are neither deep experts nor highly capable general managers.

There are few genuine experts. Expertise is rare by definition. Deep experts are a special breed. They have more focused experiences than others, and they learn more from their experience. They practice their craft more consistently than others, and their practice is more disciplined. Deep experts are passionate about their field and highly motivated by recognition of their expertise.

Those who grow into general managers are also a special breed. They tend to have broader perspectives, curiosity about a range of subjects, and may be easily bored if they're asked to stick with a particular discipline. Their technical skills are a relatively small part of their skills portfolio. They have a broad set of skills that extend to business acumen, people management skills, and operational expertise. Generalists have the ability to move from one function to another and, when they have the potential to ascend high and fast in the organization, form the ranks of our current and future general managers.

All your high potential employees have the ability to advance quickly and eventually to senior positions, but the career paths for specialists and generalists vary significantly. It's important to differentiate because specialists and generalists are developed differently, engaged differently, compensated differently, and deployed into assignments differently.

Assessing potential

Everyone has potential. Everyone has the ability to learn and grow and enhance her contribution. Genuine high potentials, though, are in short supply. It took us a while to learn to avoid false positives because we misunderstood the relationship between competence and performance

and potential. We were not unusual in that regard.
I'm convinced that many organizations do a poor job
identifying high potentials.

Virtually all of your employees will be competent and solid
performers. If they are not, why are they on your payroll?
But competence and performance are not the same as
potential.

The causal chain goes as follows. You need competence
to perform. But competence alone doesn't guarantee
performance. You need to demonstrate high performance
to qualify as a high potential. But high performance does
not guarantee potential.

Current and past performance does provide some evidence
of promotability, but it is not an accurate predictor of
who will rise to a level we'd consider top talent. There
are likely many people in your organization who deliver
excellent results but are well placed in their current position
and have limited capability for advancement. In fact, the
great majority of your high performers are not on a career
trajectory that will lead them to senior positions.

In addition to being highly competent and excellent
performers, authentic high potentials share common
characteristics. They are brighter than average—we
don't promote stupid people. They get along with
others reasonably well—we don't promote disagreeable
troublemakers. And they're highly motivated—we don't
promote people who don't care. All high potentials will
meet these three criteria in every organization. They
represent a minimum price-of-admission for advancement
to the most senior position levels.

In addition to the universal requirements, high potentials need to culturally fit with your organization, and what this means varies from one firm to another. There may be particular values that must be modeled to avoid being rejected. There may be personality traits that are tolerable in some firms, but not in yours. There may be other criteria specific to your company—ability to travel extensively, willingness to work weekends and holidays, or readiness to relocate with little notice. The price to pay for advancement to the most senior levels varies from one company to another. But the price is always high.

Importance of learning agility

Learning agility is an extremely important and often overlooked component of potential. In a nutshell, learning agility can be described as a willingness and ability to apply what's learned in one situation to another quite different situation. At face value, this seems pretty simple. It's not.

Learning agility can be considered a meta-competency that's strongly influenced by a whole raft of personality traits. No two people are identical, but those high in learning agility, those who are good at transferring what they've learned, usually share certain characteristics.

For example, very learning-agile individuals tend to be highly curious and to have broad interests. They like to experiment and don't fear making mistakes. They have a high degree of self-awareness and can read and respond to others well. They deal with stress better than most. They can't tolerate the status quo and like to lead change. And the list goes on.

There's 30 years of research underpinning learning agility that indicates this meta-competency accounts for a lot of the difference between highly successful and less successful leaders. Of course, learning agility is just one variable. Motivation, IQ, EQ, and experience also explain a lot of variance in leadership ability. But here's a key take-away: of all the factors that contribute to success, learning agility is the single most powerful predictor of success when we're considering a person who is taking on a very new and different set of responsibilities.

All jobs require some level of learning agility, just as all jobs require some degree of intelligence. And just as some jobs require more intelligence than others, some jobs require a higher degree of learning agility. In general, the need for learning agility increases as the role becomes less specialized and more generalized. Also, the need for learning agility increases as jobs become more complex, are more ambiguous, and are associated with more severe consequences.

General managers are more likely to succeed if they have a high degree of learning agility. And, as illustrated below, those who fill the most senior roles in your organization benefit from a high degree of learning agility, even if they're deep experts.

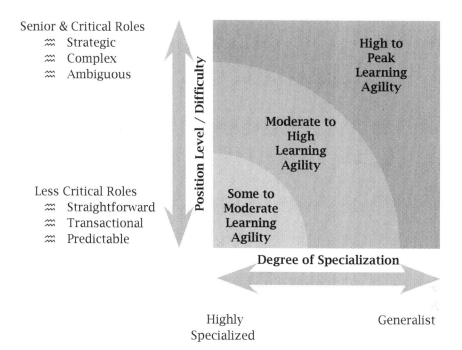

Senior & Critical Roles
- Strategic
- Complex
- Ambiguous

Less Critical Roles
- Straightforward
- Transactional
- Predictable

Position Level / Difficulty

High to Peak Learning Agility

Moderate to High Learning Agility

Some to Moderate Learning Agility

Degree of Specialization

Highly Specialized

Generalist

If all the roles in your firm are simple, transactional, predictable, and never deal with complexity, ambiguity, or urgency, you don't need to concern yourself with learning agility. It was critical for our business and likely is for yours.

When we discussed potential in our talent review, here's the definition we used to guide our discussion:

All our employees are valued contributors and have potential. Some contribute more than others. Some have more potential. High potential employees are those capable of advancing rather rapidly to senior and important positions. High potential employees may serve as generalists or follow a specialist career track. All high potential employees share certain characteristics. Without exception, they:

Serve as an exemplary model of our core values

- ☰ *Demonstrate a very high degree of intellectual horsepower*

- ☰ *Exhibit a high degree of self-awareness and emotional intelligence*

- ☰ *Are highly ambitious and driven to achieve meaningful results for the organization*

- ☰ *Relentlessly develop themselves in the competencies that matter most*

- ☰ *Possess a substantial degree of learning agility*

Applying the 9-cell performance-potential matrix

As many other companies do, we used a 9-cell performance-potential matrix in our talent reviews to guide our discussions and facilitate the differentiation of talent. When used appropriately, I've found the matrix to be very helpful. But I've seen managers struggle with its application, I think because they get so focused on figuring out the correct placement of talent in the matrix that they miss the real point. They can't decide if the person is best described as high or very high in potential. They can't quite bring themselves to put the person in the top performance category, but they seem too good to be in the middle and considered average.

Average Potential	High Potential	Very High Potential	
7 Well placed or moderate advancement	4 Significant advancement potential, perhaps to senior position	1 Fast-track with potential for royalty position	Distinctive Contributor Top Performer
8 Well placed or perhaps moderate advancement	5 Moderate advancement potential	2 Significant advancement potential to senior position	Solid Contributor Valued Performer
9 Aggressively deal with performance issues	6 Verify organizational fit; address organizational issues	3 Verify organizational fit; aggressively diagnose and develop	Marginal Contributor Performance Issues

They're missing the point. The 9-cell matrix is a framework for facilitating meaningful conversations and guiding decisions about talent. It's nothing more and nothing less. The cell placement is less important than the conversation. Meaningful conversations help us understand our inventory of talent across organizational boundaries and to make good decisions about developing and deploying individuals.

In practice, it seemed like 80% of the people we discussed would fall on a border. That's because the cells are distinct but people are not. People are complex, and everyone is different. The performance-potential matrix forced us to make comparative decisions, and that decision-making process, when accompanied by rich discussion, was very illuminating.

Here are some of our practices and points of view related to the performance-potential matrix:

≈ We made a conscious decision to not have categories for low or below-average performance or potential. On its face, I know, that sounds ridiculous. By definition, half the population is below average. But our rationale was based on the firmly held belief that our selection and management practices yielded an above-average workforce.

This is a corollary from Ivy League grading practices. The median grade awarded at Harvard, for instance, is A-. Is that grade inflation or a reflection of reality? The school has very selective admission practices and admits fewer than 10% of applicants even though the applicant pool is comprised of stellar high school students. Perhaps it's reasonable to believe that the average student at Harvard really is an A student. That's how we felt about our workforce, but I can't say that viewpoint would be realistic in other companies.

≈ We did not apply a forced distribution to the matrix and felt to do so would be counterproductive. Instead, we had well-defined criteria for each cell and worked hard to populate the matrix so it reflected the reality of our talent inventory, not some theoretically ideal distribution curve.

In practice, we had fewer than 20% of our total employee population placed in cells 1–4, and fewer than 5% in cell 1. That's just the way it turned out for us when we applied our criteria and did our best to objectively and rigorously differentiate talent. To me, that always felt right for my organization, but organizations differ. If the matrix reflects reality, the distribution will vary from company to company.

≈ Over years of experience in which I participated in hundreds of hours of talent reviews, I learned to anticipate the time required to discuss talent. My rule of thumb was an average of 15 minutes per candidate. This assumes our managers were well prepared and presented candidates quickly and objectively. It also assumes a skilled facilitator who kept us focused and on track.

We only spent five minutes on some employees. Occasionally we would spend as much as 30 minutes. We were awkward in the first couple of years and much less efficient. But once we knew what we were doing, the average was consistently 15 minutes per candidate.

≈ We generally only devoted time to discuss employees who were considered for placement in cells 1-4. In practice, we placed more candidates in cell 4 than in cells 1-3 combined. We set a high bar for potential. The right-hand column was reserved for the small number of people who could advance far more quickly than others and had a realistic shot at reaching the most senior and responsible positions in the organization.

Cell 3 was mostly reserved for those who had relatively short tenure with the organization and hadn't fully established a performance track record. If we had a tenured high potential employee who wasn't demonstrating at least solid performance, this usually required quite a bit of discussion because something serious was going on. Either we were missing something in our evaluation of the candidate or there was an organizational issue at play preventing the employee from performing. In either case, we did our best to get to the bottom of the issue and resolve it.

Preparing for talent reviews

Prior to participating in the annual talent review process, managers considered all their direct reports and did the following:

- ≋ Place direct reports on the 9-cell matrix to differentiate them according to performance and potential.

- ≋ For those in cells 1-4, document talking points to guide their presentation of each candidate in the talent review.

- ≋ Consider the readiness of each candidate for a new assignment and categorize as a) immediate—6 months, b) 6-18 months, or c) more than 18 months.

- ≋ Consider the development needs of each candidate and recommendations for next-step full-time assignments that address needed competencies and/ or needed exposures to enhance perspective.

- ≋ Consider recommendations for other development, e.g., develop-in-place assignments, coaching, etc.

- ≋ Meet with each candidate for a career conversation to better understand career goals, motivation, and engagement. Describe the talent review process, set expectations about career development, and address questions and concerns.

Talent review process

Our talent review process was pretty simple:

1. The review meetings were attended by a group of peer managers, their boss, a skilled facilitator from HR, and an assistant to the facilitator to take notes. Prior to the start of the meeting, each manager positioned their candidates on a performance-potential matrix poster using Post-it® Notes with candidate names.

2. The facilitator reviewed the ground rules and then each manager, in turn, spoke about one of their candidates. The process began with cell 1 and then proceeded through cells 2, 3, and 4. Managers, free from interruption, gave brief introductions of the candidate under review and then provided objective evidence and examples to support placement in the cell. They also stated their recommendation for readiness, next step, and development. This was done quickly and succinctly and typically would take about five minutes, sometimes even less.

3. The facilitator then asked peers who had experience with the candidate to provide additional objective evidence to support or challenge the placement. The senior manager

in the group withheld comment until the peers had weighed in.

4. Based on the nature of the conversation, the candidate might be moved to another cell at the discretion of the immediate manager. This process was repeated until all candidates had been discussed. After all candidates were reviewed, there was one more opportunity to reposition candidates.

5. Finally, we took one more pass through the candidates to further discuss, if necessary, and confirm the timing and nature of the next-step job assignment and other developmental recommendations. All decisions that had been recorded were reviewed prior to adjournment.

Talent review facilitation guidelines

Facilitating an effective talent review is much more difficult than it may seem on its face. The facilitator has to keep the meeting on point and ensure that the discussion is meaningful without getting bogged down in unimportant details.

Managers are prone to making subjective comments when presenting their candidates, and the facilitator must be insistent without being overbearing when steering the discussion to objective evidence. The facilitator must be credible and totally trustworthy. And the facilitator must manage the egos of a roomful of managers, especially the ego of the senior manager in the room. Isabel facilitated our talent reviews and did a masterful job of keeping me in line. Not an easy job.

Our reviews were guided by some ground rules:

≈ Only one person speaks at a time.

≈ This is not the place for hearsay. Provide objective evidence to support your evaluation of performance and potential and to justify recommendations.

≈ Demonstrate managerial courage. Don't sugarcoat but don't disparage. Be honest but constructive.

≈ The immediate manager is in the best position to evaluate candidates. When there's a lack of consensus or a majority disagrees with the evaluation of a candidate, the immediate manager makes the final call and accepts accountability.

≈ Unless something makes it impossible to do so, issues will be resolved in the meeting. Decisions postponed tend to get lost.

≈ Candidates have the right to know how senior leaders view them, and the immediate manager has a responsibility to provide feedback. Strict confidentiality will be maintained with regard to specific statements and individual viewpoints.

Talent review outcomes

Managers were expected to meet with their candidates after the talent review to provide feedback. The idea was to provide reinforcement and specific developmental suggestions but not to communicate specific cell placement, detailed statements about potential, or to convey the opinions of individuals. The intent was to provide constructive feedback about perceived strengths and developmental opportunities. This was an opportunity to give guidance that had the weight of a leadership team behind it.

For instance, a candidate might receive feedback summarized as follows: a) your technical skills are highly respected and valued, b) your level of business acumen, especially related to finance, is questionable, and c) you will benefit from getting out of the materials testing lab once in a while to get some exposure in operations.

This feedback would be supplemented with examples and targeted suggestions for addressing the development opportunities. The manager would answer specific questions to the extent possible and be direct but constructive in providing feedback.

Our talent reviews were perhaps the single most valuable way in which we leveraged our talent. Talent reviews increased our insight and gave us a shared understanding of our inventory of talent that spanned organizational boundaries. Talent reviews enhanced our decisions about deploying and developing talent. And talent reviews were absolutely the most effective means of educating our leaders in how to identify, develop, and deploy talent.

Deployment and development

There's not much point in differentiating talent if you're not going to act on it. Talent reviews should result in specific decisions about the role and timing of next-step assignments. These decisions comprise a dynamic succession plan that's created and documented in talent reviews, updated annually, and reviewed frequently. It's great to have a plan, but it has to be executed. You have to follow through.

Our focus was on leveraging jobs for development. We applied the 70:20:10 rule which states that we learn the most of what we need for success, roughly 70%, through experience, by doing a job. We learn about 20% from other people—bosses, coaches, peers, and significant others. And we learn about 10% from formal, event-based education and training programs. All the sources of learning are important, but jobs trump all.

Leverage the developmental power of your jobs

Since jobs provide the most opportunities for learning, it was important for us to understand the developmental power of our jobs. We put effort into analyzing jobs we felt provided significant development opportunities. It took quite a bit of work to do initially, but we studied and categorized several dozen jobs on the career paths leading to royalty positions. They were at different position levels, required different important competencies, and provided essential and unique perspectives on the business. To say that these positions required essential competencies is the same as saying they taught essential competencies. We, figuratively speaking, put revolving doors on these jobs. Every few years a new high potential moved into each of these jobs.

Of course, we needed more than several dozen developmental jobs to provide opportunities for all our employees, so all jobs were considered developmental for certain people at certain career stages. All our jobs were developmental at the right time for the right person, but we carefully managed the deployment of high potential talent into our key development jobs.

We expected our managers to delegate job-enriching assignments such as special projects for development, and we also encouraged employees to participate in extracurricular activities. Professional organizations and volunteer roles can be an excellent way to develop leadership competencies.

We had an introverted engineer who didn't get much management attention until his boss learned he was a district leader in the Boy Scouts and had major responsibilities for orchestrating the National Scout Jamboree. We promoted him to a project manager position where he excelled largely based on what he'd learned as a Scout leader. Every month, we included a short article in our employee newsletter to highlight an employee who was benefitting from this type of experience.

Assessments and coaching

Our assessment and coaching strategy was an important part of development and integrated with our succession planning. We established a small group of internal coaches and, for senior people, also used several external coaches to provide assessment feedback. All of our employees received 360 feedback every three years, but our high potentials were assessed annually and provided formal feedback on the assessment results.

Our assessment strategy for high potentials used three different assessments: a 360 competency assessment, a personality assessment that included career derailers, and a specialized assessment of emotional intelligence. Each year, one-third of the high potential population was administered one of these three assessments. The groups rotated each year to be assessed with a different assessment. Individualized feedback and coaching was provided after every assessment. We documented the schedule for each candidate in our talent reviews.

Rater anonymity was protected for the 360 assessment, and results were kept confidential and only seen by the employee and the coach. However, HR received assessment data for the other two assessments (which were not multi-rater assessments) and reviewed those with the immediate manager. Assessment results were typically not shared in talent reviews, but they were available to supplement and potentially validate our evaluation of potential.

Rate of advancement

You want to advance your fast-track high potential employees through developmental positions as quickly as possible but not so quickly that you short-circuit key lessons provided by the experience. The learning curve for most positions filled by high potentials starts flattening out after one year, but I've found that it's usually a good idea to leave an employee in a role for at least two years before moving them on to their next assignment.

Often the mistakes we make in the first year don't come back to bite us until well into the second year, and if you move people too soon, you may deprive them of learning from their mistakes. On the other hand, if you leave high potential talent in a position for more than three years, you're likely to waste time.

My suggestion is to move high potentials every two and a half to three years, but this is only an average. Some jobs have a tough learning curve and may need three or four years or more in order to wring the learning value from the experience. It's also possible there are roles assigned to expand perspective by providing exposures to different customer segments, regions, or other aspects of the business. Often those perspectives can be gained in less than two years.

My suggestions on rate of advancement apply primarily to high potential generalists. I'll provide additional thoughts about developing high potential specialists in the next chapter. In short, the primary difference in advancement rates is that generalists typically move through positions more rapidly and have much greater variety in the types of assignments than specialists.

Transparency

Don't make this difficult. My suggestion is to be absolutely transparent about the process for differentiating talent and the application of differential treatment. I do not recommend that you create "high potential lists" or feel the need to tell candidates they are high potentials. The reasons are several.

First of all, your high potentials already know they're high potentials because you're treating them differently. They're getting more attention. You're giving them more responsibility, stretching them more, and advancing them more rapidly. An employee who is indeed high potential certainly doesn't need anyone to tell them so—they already know it.

Also, labeling an employee as a high potential can create a sense of entitlement. Success must be earned every step along the career path, and there's no such thing as a permanent status. People sometimes disappoint us. It's possible that the person who stood out in last year's talent review has hit a ceiling or derailed this year. Hopefully, that's a rare occurrence, but the point is that there is no room for conferring status that may be perceived as permanent.

Be clear about your talent management practices and your intent to develop talent aggressively based on your current and best understanding of their potential and contribution. And nothing more.

Proactively manage careers

If you take a hands-off approach with the careers of your high potentials and allow them to self-select into jobs, you won't have internal candidates ready to fill royalty positions when you need them. Not unless you're incredibly lucky.

Most people won't self-select into the jobs that are most developmental. You need to be proactive and make those decisions for them. Or at least with them. I'm not suggesting you create an environment in which they feel coerced.

Actually, I've seen that it's quite engaging for high potentials when you help them understand how careers are built and the reason they're receiving the tough assignment is because the organizations cares about them enough to give them the assignments that will be most valuable to their long-term career success.

149

The most developmental jobs are those that are very different from previous jobs, that are seen as undesirable, and that have severe consequences for failure. Every high potential should have at least one or two jobs like this in their career. Help them see the value in such assignments.

Hoarding talent

When a manager has a stellar employee, it's natural they want to hang on to them. One of my responsibilities was to make it clear that talent did not belong to a department or business unit. Talent belonged to the enterprise.

The hoarding of talent more often raised its ugly head when it was time to execute a decision, less often at the time the decision was made. It typically happened like this. During a talent review, a decision was made to assign Sally to manage a large complex team in Sam's business unit in six months when the current team leader was moving on. It was exactly the kind of assignment that Sally needed, and everyone agreed. However, when the time came, Sam had someone else in mind, a favorite candidate from his unit.

It always pissed me off when I had to get in the middle of this kind of situation, but in the early days it was sometimes necessary in order to set clear expectations and create the kind of organizational culture we needed. If the decisions made in a talent review are made thoughtfully and seriously, there better be a damn good reason for not following through on them.

Managing risk

At the beginning of this chapter, I talked about the dilemma we face in succession. If we deploy people into jobs in which they lack capability, they put our business at risk. And if we deploy people into jobs for which they're already fully capable, they'll have limited opportunity to develop. We considered the risk when making deployment decisions and took actions to mitigate it.

As an example, we had a young lady, an engineer, who was considered to be very high potential and on a fast track to a senior position. Sarah was in her early 30s and had already worked for us for ten years in a series of four jobs. She excelled in all of them to the extent I felt I'd never really seen her challenged. I wanted to know what she was really capable of accomplishing and suggested we assign her to lead an upcoming, high visibility and risky project with our biggest customer.

When I made the suggestion, it created a bit of a stir in the talent review. The widespread sentiment was that Sarah was too junior to take on such an important role and had never managed anything approaching the complexity of the project.

We took two significant actions to address the concerns. The first was to provide a safety net by assigning Bill, a vice president, to monitor the project closely but discreetly. Bill was highly experienced and would have been a natural choice to ramrod the project. Instead, his assignment was to keep his hands off and only engage with Sarah if she appeared to be sinking. We knew she'd be in over her head, but we wanted to give her a chance to figure out how to swim.

The second action we took was to have a conversation with Sarah to discuss the assignment. I actually took part in the conversation with Sarah and her immediate manager. We told her we had an opportunity for her that was going to stretch her like she'd never been stretched before. We gave her some suggestions for getting started on the right foot and expressed confidence that she could be successful and that we wouldn't assign the project to her if we thought she was going to fail. Although it probably wasn't necessary, we impressed upon her the importance of the project.

We did not tell Sarah that Bill was going to be monitoring things. We did not tell her that she needn't worry, that Bill would ride in on a white horse to pull her ass out of the fire if she got in trouble. We wanted her to feel the heat, to feel the pressure, but also to sense that we were invested in her success and had confidence in her.

Today Sarah is a vice president and will be running a company someday, mine or another. I have no doubt. That's what succession planning can do for you.

Cedric, the theater manager, is experiencing something similar. His assignment probably doesn't have the same significance for the cruise line as Sarah's assignment had for my company. But I can tell you that Cedric was challenged, stretched, and will move on to his next position armed with new competencies, invigorated self-confidence, and an accelerated career trajectory.

Leading Innovation

Day 7: January 5th, Caribbean Sea

Last night was a good time. There was an open-air chess exhibition on an upper deck, and a grandmaster played 20 volunteers simultaneously. He soundly thrashed 19 players and drew with one—me!

Betsy had signed me up without my knowledge, and when I learned of it, I was sure I would be crushed and embarrassed. Instead, I now have one more story with which I'll be able to bore unsuspecting cocktail party guests. Don't worry, I won't provide you with a move-by-move replay of his Queen's Gambit (which I wisely declined), but I will recount an incident which occurred during the exhibition.

The grandmaster—first name Yuri, last name unpronounceable—moved rapidly from board to board. I rarely had more than three or four minutes between moves, which meant he was averaging about ten seconds for each of his moves. Fortunately, he played the only opening that I know moderately well, and I was somehow able to keep up.

Midway through the game, a drunk passenger began causing a bit of a disturbance. He lurched around the outside of the ring of seated players trying to keep pace with the grandmaster who was shuffling between boards on the inside of the ring. The drunk, who was sporting only outlandish tattoos and an obscene Speedo, had a hard time keeping up with Yuri because there was a bit of a crowd behind the seated players watching the games. Being drunk didn't help Speedo navigate or make articulate comments.

Speedo was jostling people and making rude comments directed at the grandmaster, but I have to say, they seemed to have no effect on the champion's ability to concentrate. I always thought elite chess players were persnickety and temperamental, but Yuri, who appeared to be about 20 years old, had the concentration of Buddha.

Then it happened. We were 15 or 20 moves into the game when Speedo lumbered up directly behind the player to my left and leaned forward to give some pointers. His balance was no better than his knowledge of chess, and the guy stumbled and knocked the board over. A couple of security guys, who'd been gradually working their way over to intervene, finally jumped into action and quickly removed the mischief-maker and, with him, the offensive swimwear.

Without hesitation, Yuri picked up the fallen chessboard and swiftly and effortless reset the chess pieces. We all watched, amazed that he could apparently hold 20 chess games in his head simultaneously, that he could track the placement of 640 pieces on 1,280 squares more easily than I can remember my own anniversary.

When he was finished, Yuri asked his opponent, "Does it look right to you?"

It was right, of course, and Yuri resumed play without missing a beat and thus destroyed any shred of confidence possessed by his opponents. I, too, felt my confidence flag, but my stubbornness remained intact, and there was no way I was going to lie down. I focused and just played defensively.

In the end, he offered me a draw when we were each holding a minor piece and three opposed pawns. He had a knight to my white bishop, and I'm convinced he could have pretty easily used his knight to gain a pawn advantage and win outright. I don't know why he offered a draw. Maybe he was just taking pity on an old man, but I didn't think twice and gladly accepted his offer and shook his extended hand.

So this morning I woke in a good mood, kissed Betsy, and thanked her for insisting that I go on the cruise. On this voyage I've dined with other CEOs, had a guided island tour from a 10-year-old entrepreneur, witnessed an unforgettable stage disaster, played a chess grandmaster to a draw, and done a considerable amount of writing. All in all, not a bad week.

And now, on my last full day at sea, I am writing about innovation, a topic I've held in reserve for my final chapter. So far I've focused on talent. If talent is the foundation, innovation is the capstone.

Innovation is an incredibly important topic for anyone running a business. Innovation is driven by talent, especially talent that possesses deep expertise. That's why the chess story relates. Yuri is a deep expert, and innovation is driven by deep expertise.

There are lots of books and articles written about innovation, and I've read many of them. None seem to capture the primary lesson that I've learned about innovation: expertise, more than any other factor, determines your ability to innovate.

I know what you're thinking. Duh! That's not a lesson. Of course you need expertise to innovate. Yeah, well it must not be that obvious because so many books on innovation gloss over or completely ignore the role of expertise and instead focus on getting the right culture, recruiting diverse teams, implementing gate reviews and process metrics, taking risk, and celebrating failure. A lot of what's written about innovation is, in my estimation, just so much twaddle.

Look, there's no such thing as the perfect culture to drive innovation. Even if there was a perfect innovation culture, it wouldn't guarantee innovation. The power of team diversity is over-rated. In fact, diversity may work against you. And go ahead, use gate reviews, take risks, celebrate failure, and do a great job measuring everything. Good luck. It doesn't mean you'll innovate.

But if you do nothing other than assemble a handful of engaged experts—I'm talking true experts—you've at least got a shot at innovation.

Innovation drives business success

To innovate is to create and implement something new and different. Innovation is a fresh approach to solving a problem and application of the solution. Innovation is both thinking and doing. Innovation is follow through, the commercialization of a good idea.

Innovation is vital because it's the only way you can reliably achieve profitable growth. And profitable growth is the chief objective of every CEO. You've got to have profit. That goes without saying. But profit is not enough. You also need growth. In a dynamic competitive landscape, the company that's not growing is on its way to irrelevance.

There are really only two ways to grow. One, you can grab a bigger slice of the pie by stealing business from the competition. It's fun if you can do it. But it's not easy. Two, you can grow the pie. Innovation in products and services may do both. Innovative products and services can grow the market. They can grow the pie. And innovative products and services can also snare your competitor's customers and enlarge your piece of the pie.

In addition, process innovation can grow your profitability because it means you're running your business more effectively. Less time. Less scrap. Less friction. Less cash consumed. More cash remaining. More to the bottom line. That's wealth. And it's the job of the CEO to create wealth. It's the job of the CEO to drive innovation.

Above all, innovation requires expertise

We can all cite accidental discoveries that have launched groundbreaking innovations. But if we're serious about innovation, we can't wait for accidents. We have to be intentional about it, and that means we need experts.

Experts have the ability to see anomalies that others don't. They see similarities others miss. They see connections that are invisible to non-experts. They see patterns. And it's those patterns and connections that are the basis of innovation.

Yuri was able to reset the chessboard not because he remembered the location of 64 individual chess pieces. He tracked patterns rather than pieces. Yuri could look around the circle of opponents and see each game in progress represented as a pattern as easily as we might look at a group of 20 people and see a long-sleeve blue shirt here, short-sleeve white shirt there, and a paisley print between.

Innovation comes from the connections experts see between patterns. The first step to becoming intentional about innovation is to understand experts and the nature of expertise. Here's what I've learned about experts:

> ≈ *Experts are passionate about their discipline.* They are more than highly interested. They are more than hobbyists. Experts are focused, obsessive, and single-minded in a way that's nearly incomprehensible to the non-expert. They are driven to study, think, experiment, and to develop their own unique point of view that is the result of their own work. Ownership is important to them. They cultivate their passion and fiercely guard their expertise because they've invested so much in it. They own it. In fact, that largely explains why they are so passionate. Passion builds as expertise builds. Passion sounds a lot like engagement, doesn't it?

> ≈ *Experts have a vast amount of experience.* The passion of experts leads them to spend more quality time working in their discipline. The 10,000 hour rule was identified in research years ago and popularized more recently by Malcolm Gladwell. The point is that, although there are ways to accelerate and enhance the value of experience, there is really no way to get around the sizable investment in time required to develop expertise. A true expert in any recognized discipline—chess player, diesel mechanic, or physician—has paid their dues.

> ≈ *The nature of an expert's experience is different.* It's not just that experts have more

experience, there's a qualitative difference in their experience. They practice differently. It's more focused, more intentional, more mindful. It leads the expert musician player to play the same four bars of difficult music over and over and over again until it's more than perfect, until it's natural. As martial artist Bruce Lee said, "I fear not the man who has practiced 10,000 kicks once, but I fear the man who has practiced one kick 10,000 times." It leads a grandmaster chess player like Yuri to not just practice lots of different openings, but to intently practice the Queen's Gambit Declined hundreds (perhaps thousands) of times.

≈ *An expert's motives are different.* They are achievement-oriented, but the way they define achievement is different from others. More than anything else, they are motivated by being an expert. They love to have answers that others don't. They love to be in demand for what they know. That's not to say that experts don't have other motivators. They may value autonomy, money, power, security, or affiliation, for instance. But above all, they long to breathe the rare air that only true experts breathe when they reach the pinnacle of their profession.

To drive innovation, we also need to understand the nature of expertise so we can nurture it in our organizations. Our knowledge of expertise will help us to better develop and engage deep experts. So here's what I've learned:

≈ *Deep expertise is rare.* Most everyone has some level of expertise in one thing or another. There are a lot of expert wannabees. But the truth is, there are very, very few true experts. Deep experts stand head and shoulders above others in their command of their discipline. They have the passion, experience, and motivation discussed above, and that combination has created something truly special.

Never underestimate what it takes to develop authentic deep expertise or the value it provides. Once I was in a long meeting with four highly skilled tool designers who were working on a particularly challenging problem involving part geometry. Randy, our authentic deep expert, entered the room and within ten minutes saw the solution that had eluded the team of very competent engineers who'd been studying the problem for hours. Like all true experts, Randy made his craft appear easy. I could give you a dozen similar examples. The contribution of a true expert may be worth the combined contribution of 20 others who are merely competent.

≈ *Expertise changes the way problems are solved.* Many are prone to think that experts find the best solutions because they're analytical and use a disciplined approach to problem solving. No. At the risk of spouting what should be self-evident, the best problem solvers are simply those who know the most about the subject. Pure and simple. Experts know the most. Their experience has provided them with many stored patterns that are the source of their intuition. It's non-experts who typically resort to analysis and structured problem solving. Intelligence can be thought of as the ability to recognize patterns and to draw inferences and make predictions based on those patterns. That's what experts do.

≈ *Expertise is transparent to the expert.* Experts typically have a high degree of unconscious competence. They don't know everything they know. They just know. They often can't explain how they see solutions that others miss. The answers just appear, almost magically. Their stored mental models and patterns are incredibly rich, and focused practice has carved deep neural networks that enable solutions to spring forth clearly and unobstructed. When Yuri looked at a chessboard last night, he wasn't analyzing. He was just recognizing a pattern and then, typically within a couple of seconds, selecting the move that had wondrously jumped to his consciousness.

≋ *For the most part, deep expertise is tacit.* Because it's transparent to the expert, it's virtually impossible for the expert to articulate. Imagine you pose a problem to an expert and ask them to speak aloud as they solve the problem so you can understand how they reach a solution. Forget it. As quickly as you can describe the problem, the expert's brain is scanning (probably subconsciously) patterns stored from experience and identifying a preferred solution. But since the request was to articulate the thought process, the expert will attempt to explain the intuited solution by implying some analysis or decision-making process that might sound good but that totally fails to capture what's really happened in the brain.

This phenomenon presents a real dilemma to those of us who would like to capture and document and disseminate expertise. If your organization develops the capability to transform the tacit to the explicit, you're on your way to building a capacity for innovation.

≈ *Multiplying expertise is difficult.* OK, let's be honest. It's more than difficult. It's a bitch. Because expertise is rare and largely defines one's value to an organization, asking an expert to share expertise represents a threat of sorts. If I share my expertise, won't it reduce my value? Now, many experts do rise above this and may even fail to recognize it, but the threat is there nonetheless and may complicate the transfer of expertise.

Remember that experts are motivated by being an expert. Recognition for expertise is fertilizer for the ego, and many experts have outsized egos. Those egos can be a huge problem. Egos confound teamwork, listening, teaching, cooperation, fairness, understanding, sharing, negotiation, humor, and relationships in general. When you try to multiply expertise in your organization, you'll face all these obstacles and more.

Support the expert career path

If deep experts are the drivers of innovation, we need to understand how their expertise is developed, how their careers are built. Career support is an engagement driver, a driver that most organizations fail to fully leverage. Those organizations that do define career paths and provide career support often focus on the generalist path. Few provide sufficient definition, branding, and support for the technical career path. But it's your pool of technical specialists that provides the talent most likely to drive innovation in your organization. Here's what I've learned about supporting the careers of technical talent, in particular, high potential specialists:

≈ *Build depth in the discipline.* Unlike generalists who typically have a variety of roles in their careers, experts normally stay within a narrowly defined discipline and career track. They may take one or two short assignments outside of their function over the course of their career, but this is relatively rare for deep experts.

The roles of deep experts are narrower and the positions are also stickier. Experts move between roles less frequently than do generalists. Even those who are on a fast track for advancement will stay in their roles for longer time periods as a specialist. The high potential generalist may be moving to a new position every two or three years, often making a lateral move. High potential specialists may stay in a position for four or five years. The reason for this has less to do with the length of learning curves than it has to do with availability of roles within a function. But specialists still need to be aggressively developed in jobs just as generalists do.

To accomplish this, we had to get creative and introduce a variety of developmental stretch assignments for our deep experts. We often assigned short-term special projects that placed our experts outside of their comfort zone. Sometimes we were able to "lend" them to key clients to work on projects that stretched the expert, directly benefited our customer, and provided us with long-term benefit. We also periodically created pilot projects to explore applications of our technology to new markets— healthcare, for instance.

≈ *Develop teaching/coaching skills.* Stretch your technical experts by pushing them into coaching and teaching roles. These roles can be formal or informal, but the important thing is to get them accustomed to sharing, to talking about the specifics of what they do. There's an old saying that you never really know something until you've taught it to someone else.

Since expertise is transparent, experts find it very difficult to share their tacit heuristics. Sure, they may be able to talk about the general technology or discipline, the stuff typically found in related textbooks. But can they articulate their heuristics, their rules of thumb, their tricks of the trade? In this, they will most assuredly struggle, yet this is a primary way to grow and multiply organizational expertise.

Experts will often benefit from having a coach, especially a coach to help enhance their self-awareness and emotional intelligence, but don't neglect the opportunity to cast them in the role of a coach. We assigned high potential specialists to coach emerging talent and reaped multiple benefits. Young, energetic high potentials want to learn about how the organization works, how careers are built, elements of the business strategy, customer insights, and so on. They do need to learn these things, but they also need to learn about the technology and expertise that drive the organization's value proposition and fuel innovation.

The young high potentials pushed our experts to think more deeply about organizational issues, develop perspective, and enhance emotional intelligence. The experts pushed the young high potentials to learn technical aspects of the business. The coaching relationship benefited both parties.

≋ *Develop perspective.* Experts are focused on their discipline and stick to a narrow career path. Nothing wrong with that as long as they don't develop tunnel vision to a point that they're unaware of business challenges, the competitive landscape, customer segments, and business fundamentals. You don't need to jump to a different career track to gain perspective.

We ensured that our experts occasionally visited customers and served on cross-functional project teams tasked with tackling organizational issues. This gave them opportunity to learn how the business works and develop relationships outside of their discipline. Ensure your experts are not insulated or isolated from the broader organization. Make sure they have opportunity to develop a degree of perspective that will enhance their deep expertise.

≋ *Leverage external development opportunities.* Encourage your experts to participate in professional activities outside of the organization. Support them in those activities. Experts will find it stimulating and engaging to participate in professional societies and conferences. You want them to be more than passive attendees, though, and it's OK to push them outside of their comfort zone.

We strongly encouraged our experts to make presentations, submit journal articles, lead panel discussions, and serve in leadership roles. Remember that development occurs outside of our comfort zone, and we wanted our experts to become skillful in articulating what they know. Proprietary expertise, of course, was off limits, but that still left lots of latitude for our technical specialists to make professional contributions. You'll find an added benefit is that experts often return from those experiences inspired and anxious to try something new that will spark innovation inside your organization.

≈ *Enhance self-awareness.* The first step to development is awareness. Without self-awareness, we won't be motivated to pursue development. We need awareness of our weaknesses, awareness of our preferences, and awareness of how others perceive us. We need to have our blind spots illuminated. Self-awareness is a critical component of emotional intelligence, which enables us to build effective relationships. It is critical for your experts.

Becoming self-aware can be a painful process, and especially so for your deep experts. They are successful. They have confidence. They may be arrogant. Figuratively speaking, we need to hold up a mirror for them to gain insight and grow in self-awareness. We addressed this with formal assessments, 360s for all employees every three years, and a cadre of internal coaches. But more importantly, we worked hard to develop coaching skills in our people managers so they could provide constructive feedback while minimizing the sense of threat that generates defensiveness.

≈ *Focus development on emotional intelligence.* The ability to manage emotions and build relationships is a strong predictor of success.

And the lack of EQ is an even stronger predictor of derailment. When your experts disappoint you, it's almost always because of relationship problems. They may find it difficult to relate to others. They may be unable to coach effectively. Worse, they may be obstinate, arrogant, uncooperative, defensive, tactless, ... and the list goes on. These problems are due to a lack of EQ skills.

The greatest gift you can provide your experts is help with developing emotional intelligence. They probably don't need much help developing their technical skills and expertise. They're capable and self-motivated learners when it concerns their area of expertise. But when it comes to relationships, it's a different story. Provide EQ development for all your employees, but especially with your specialists. We did this by periodically administering an EQ assessment and providing feedback and coaching for our experts.

≋ *Respect the importance of personal influence.* Personal influence is an engagement driver and especially important for high potential specialists. Nothing wrong with providing awards, public recognition, even monetary incentives. But remember, experts are motivated by being the expert. It's hard to top the recognition value of simply asking them for their opinion.

Talk to your deep experts. Listen closely. Learn to know them personally. Consult them frequently. Help them to learn how to influence by reinforcing appropriate behaviors and providing course-correction coaching when they exhibit inappropriate behaviors.

I had a 35-year-old materials engineering specialist, Curtis, who was a technical genius but could sometimes be a complete ass. He always had a hunch or an opinion on every topic and wasn't shy about sharing. When Curtis spoke to his area of expertise, he was an oracle. On any topic other than materials engineering, Curtis was a crackpot.

I made Curtis my personal project and started by sitting down and leveling with him. I told him what I thought of him—that he was a technical genius but totally lacking credibility outside of his area of expertise. I told him the way he presented his wide range of ideas was hurting his overall reputation and that I needed him to learn how to influence others effectively. For several years we had frequent conversations. I recognized him and provided reinforcement when he influenced effectively. I provided feedback and course correction when he didn't. I gave him lots and lots of examples and non-examples.

Now, ten years later, Curtis is on the executive team and the most influential person in the organization when it comes to innovation. He provides focus, nurtures good ideas, and helps people learn from the not-so-good ideas. Curtis has learned how to effectively exercise his influence, and I hope every one of my deep experts can learn to do the same.

≈ *Modify compensable factors as needed.* Compensation is normally calculated using several factors that may unduly short-change your deep experts, factors such as budgetary responsibility and span of control for direct and indirect reports. Your deep experts may work as individual contributors and provide value that far exceeds what can be inferred from traditional comp factors or position level or title. Consider how you may need to modify your comp calculations for targeted positions.

The problem occurs when a high potential specialist looks around the organization and sees that the general managers and sales people are reaping the largest monetary rewards. You don't want your deep experts trying to jump from their specialist career path to a generalist path because they feel their sense of fairness violated. Give this some serious consideration before you lose deep experts.

Experts need teams

Technical experts drive innovation. Never underestimate the importance of the individual expert. But teams also play an important role. Because innovation is the creation of the new and different, innovation activities are big. They require creativity, problem solving, and execution. This is typically way more than one individual can handle.

You can't innovate without technical expertise. You won't innovate without effective innovation teams. The composition of the team and selection of the team leader are critical. Here's what I've learned about leading effective teams for innovation:

> ≈ *Pay attention to the composition of your innovation teams.* Ask ten people what makes the more effective team, a diverse team or a homogenous team. Nine times out of ten (or more), the response will be the diverse team. That's not correct. At least not totally correct.

The most effective and easiest to manage teams are comprised of people with shared values and who genuinely like and respect each other. You want dysfunction in a team? Just throw a bunch of people together who have different values and see what happens. The different perspectives might, *might* lead to great creativity. But innovation is more than creativity.

Effective innovation teams are comprised of deep experts with shared values, complementary specialties, and each with enough perspective to connect with the others. They benefit from diversity of expertise, different specialties. And it's where the specialties intersect that the magic happens. When deep experts connect, innovation follows.

Bottom line: the most functional and productive innovation teams are comprised of deep experts that have diversity of expertise and experience but share similar values. They like and respect each other, and contribute equally.

≋ *The team leader plays a critical role in the innovation team, the most important role.* Peter Drucker likened managers to both the composer and the conductor of a symphony orchestra. I like this analogy when considering the role of the leader of an innovation team. Imagine an orchestra conductor dealing with all those great musicians, each one a deep expert. Each musician has spent thousands of hours practicing alone in their studio apartment, playing the same piece over and over, seeing patterns in the score, and building the muscle memory that enables them to play so effortlessly. The conductor must have credibility and a high degree of skill to get all those experts to play well together.

So it is with the leader of an innovation team. They must manage the egos of deep experts and get them to play nicely together. They can't do this unless they've got considerable emotional intelligence to build relationships with and between the team members. They must manage their own ego and be comfortable in their own skin in order to set the right tone, to create a team environment that is safe and non-threatening.

The most creative and productive atmosphere is charged with energy, animated, engaging. An oppressive atmosphere kills creativity and productivity. Effective use of humor, especially the team leader's self-deprecating humor, can help set the mood that fosters creativity.

Perhaps the biggest challenge of leading an innovation team (assuming you've done a good job of assembling experts with complementary specialties) is creating an environment in which it's safe to make mistakes. That is easier said than done. Remember that experts, above all else, want to be recognized as the expert. Imagine the group dynamics in a team of experts.

Each is likely to feel a desire to be recognized as the expert among experts, some more than others. In that environment, some will hold back in order to avoid a misstep that would mar their reputation. Others will be aggressive and tend to dominate. The team leader can't allow either to happen.

The best team leaders are adept at reading the team members and knowing when and how to encourage reserved team members and subdue the grandstanders. The goal is a team in which there is equal participation and contribution from all.

Innovation team leaders need credibility with their expert team members to win their trust. The symphony conductor may not be able to rival the skills of any individual expert musician in the orchestra on any particular instrument, but the conductor may be the most versatile musician and have familiarity with many instruments. Like the conductor, the team leader must have at least a basic understanding of the specialties represented on the team. At a minimum, team leaders must be conversant with their expert team members. They must speak the same language.

≋ *Lay the foundation with trust and shared goals.* No team will be productive unless team members have trust and confidence in each other and share common goals. Addressing these issues is the first and most important job of the team leader, and what I've previously shared about these topics in the chapter on engagement apply here. These are important enough, though, to reinforce.

Creating trust isn't always easy and should be the starting point to create team effectiveness. You can't really trust someone you don't know. You can't have much confidence in someone who's unfamiliar. The team leader needs to help team members get to know each other on a personal level. This isn't natural for most deep experts who are often introverted.

Introversion contributes to building expertise. Experts need time alone to practice, reflect, and develop their unique expert point of view. The time experts spend alone is essential to building their expertise and innovation capability. But introverts have their challenges. They are generally uncomfortable initiating conversations, especially conversations of a personal nature. Leaders of innovation teams have their work cut out for them when it comes to building relationships within the team so members trust and have confidence in each other.

Our team leaders were taught to kick off each new team with a get-acquainted activity followed by an in-depth discussion of the mission and goals of the team. When new teams convened with members who were not well acquainted, the team leader paired them up and asked them to share two things with their partner: 1) take four or five minutes to talk about someone whom you care about deeply, and 2) share an embarrassing story about yourself, the most embarrassing thing you're willing to share. After about ten minutes when everyone had an opportunity to share, the team leader would share this same personal information with the entire team.

Think about what this activity accomplishes. Asking team members to talk about someone else makes it easier for them to open up. When they talk about someone they care about, it provides personal insight and helps their partner learn about them on a fairly intimate level. Sharing something embarrassing is a way to let down defenses, lighten the mood, and send a message that it's OK to make mistakes and even to look foolish.

The way the team leader facilitates this activity and personally shares will really set the tone and help define the team's culture. I've led this activity many times and can tell you that, as uncomfortable as it is to share something embarrassing, it sends a clear signal that none of us should take ourselves too seriously. This can be a breakthrough for uptight experts who are nervous joining a team of other experts and concerned about protecting their image.

Drucker compared the manager to a composer as well as a conductor, and it's the composer role that applies to goal alignment. Just as the composer defines the time signature and melody, the innovation team leader defines and clarifies the team's goals.

You can't assume there's alignment with the goals just because they've been clearly communicated. The leader must facilitate team discussion of the goals. The team leader may need to check in with individual team members to identify concerns and points of misalignment. Make this a top priority with every team that's formed. Create buy-in to the team's goals. Create alignment. Verify it. Reinforce it.

☰ *Create urgency without creating threat.*
The innovation team leader role is very demanding. In addition to the ability to build relationships and manage the egos of a group of deep experts, the leader needs to be skilled at organizing and measuring work, managing processes, and driving for results.

In my experience, the leaders who focus on achievement and send positive messages are far more effective than those who focus on avoiding failure and are in the habit of using threatening messages. This seems like it should be intuitive, but it always surprised me how many team leaders, especially first-time team leaders, think they have to be a hard-ass to be a good leader.

For deep experts, the nastiest threat is a threat to their ego, to their status as an expert. Each will want to establish and maintain a favorable position in their team of peers, and an insensitive team leader can unwittingly devastate an expert by criticizing them publicly, dismissing their contribution, or simply ignoring them.

I'm not saying leaders don't need to be tough. I'm not saying that sometimes they don't have to be a bit of a hard-ass. They sometimes do. But they should demonstrate their toughness appropriately and in a way that doesn't threaten the expert team members who are the ultimate drivers of team success. This may entail private conversations with team members, but at a minimum, it requires that team leaders carefully consider the messages they send, especially when conversations are public.

≋ *Promote constructive conflict.* The best innovation teams are not collaborative. Not in the traditional sense. When Joe shares an idea, Jane makes a suggestion, Jean adds an input, and then everything gets mushed up in a compromise, the result is almost always a sub-optimal solution.

The best innovation teams debate. They compete. They argue. They don't settle. They don't compromise on sub-optimal solutions. And they can do this all constructively because they respect each other, they like each other, and they're united by a shared goal to create and implement something new and different and exciting.

When my brothers and I were kids, we used to beat the crap out of each other in the morning but be best friends by the afternoon. We still sometimes argue like hell when we go on fishing trips. But we're still brothers, always brothers. I don't want to overstate this, but the best innovation teams have the feel of a family. Members can disagree, can argue without damaging relationships. In a family, it's because of familial love. In an innovation team, it's because of deep respect for each other's expertise and contribution.

The team leader is responsible for creating an environment in which it's safe to disagree, to stand alone, to debate. It's got to be safe to make mistakes. That doesn't mean mistakes are celebrated. It means that team members don't take themselves so seriously that they hold back or exhibit negative and unproductive behavior. It starts with a team leader that models the right behavior and reinforces it in team members.

Senior leadership plays a key role in innovation

The contribution of deep experts working independently and in teams led by a skilled leader is the stuff of innovation. Capable experts and team leaders are essential, but senior organizational leadership has a huge part to play in driving innovation.

The most important responsibilities include everything I've written about talent in the preceding pages. Senior leadership needs to recruit, align, engage, develop, and deploy talent. Innovation is next to impossible without the right talent management strategy and execution.

Senior leadership also has very important responsibilities related to providing focus, dedicating resources, defining risk, and shaping the organizational culture. Here's what I learned about the role I played as CEO of an innovative organization:

~~~ *Be intentional about culture.* Our culture is simply the collective normal behaviors we exhibit at work. The way we do our jobs, solve problems, communicate, hire, fire, celebrate, dress, and even park our vehicles are a reflection of our culture. When norms of behavior are narrowly defined, we say we have a strong culture. When there's a lot of latitude given to behaviors in the organization, it indicates a weak culture.

Behaviors are a reflection of our values and assumptions about how the world works. Values are important and should be selected to drive behaviors that are aligned with our strategy. It's a primary responsibility of senior leadership, especially the CEO, to define the values that are important to the organization.

It's not the job of employees or anyone else to define organizational values. Senior leaders who don't define and clearly explain the values that are important and the behaviors that reflect those values are, simply stated, shirking their responsibility.

Innovation can occur within a wide range of cultures, but there a couple of attributes that are prevalent in innovative organizations:

1. In most innovative organizations, relationships are informal and leaders are approachable. Even if there are many levels in a complex structure, employees feel free to interact with leaders at all levels. A high level of approachability is typical in innovative organizations.

2. Related to approachability, the second cultural attribute common in innovative organizations is freedom of expression. Employees not only feel free to approach and interact with leaders at all levels, they also are free to challenge and disagree. A punitive culture that squashes dissent will squash innovation.

As CEO, I made an effort to frequently share my values and identify behaviors that were aligned with those values. I tried to model approachability and insisted on this in my managers. And I thanked employees when they spoke up and challenged and even disagreed with me. I did this publicly and, to the best of my ability, authentically.

There was only one time in an all-hands meeting in which I had to shut an employee down, but I tried to do it in a way that recognized the value of dissent. Clifford was a valued employee but opinionated and vocal. In one meeting, he repeatedly asked for the mike to ask questions and voice opinions. It reached a point that I had to intervene; I thanked him publicly for his engagement and contribution but told him we'd have to take it off line in fairness to everyone else. I didn't want this to discourage others and told my employees that I wanted to hear more from Clifford, but I also wanted to hear from others too.

≋ *Focus innovation efforts.* As the CEO, I could give direction to my innovation teams and set some high-level goals, but it usually wasn't possible to get very specific. The nature of innovation is such that there is a lot of ambiguity about even the problems, let alone the solutions. What I could do was provide focus on a particular customer issue, production problem, or market opportunity.

For example, I could launch a team to find a way to reduce weight and simplify assembly of the coaxial rotor drive in a particular model of helicopter. Although this sounds like the problem is defined, it's really not. There's a lot of ambiguity that the team will have to deal with even in the problem statement. They will have to really understand the problem, why it's important to the customer, and identify many related issues that will impact possible solutions. Innovation is an exercise in problem solving, and problem solving is an exercise in dealing with ambiguity.

I could further provide a sense of urgency by being specific about targets related to quality and efficiency, but especially related to time and cost. For instance, I could communicate to the team that in order for us to participate in the upcoming CR2 program, we need to be ready on September 1st to demonstrate how we can reduce the weight of the coaxial rotor drive by 20% and reduce assembly time by 30%.

What's important is that I provide focus and create a sense of urgency by setting some targets. There should always be focus, but sometimes the goals can be blurry. For instance, I might choose to launch an innovation team that is directed to work on generating new business with our helicopter customers. The team may be given a wide field with ill-defined borders in which to identify opportunities and develop solutions.

Senior leadership should create a sense of urgency and focus on innovation. Focus is important, but don't be so focused that there is no slack or freedom to pursue unexpected opportunities that arise. The way you dedicate and distribute resources should back up your messages about what's important. Resources and focus can't be separated, and resources are necessary to provide some slack and freedom to benefit innovation.

≈ *Organize for innovation.* You also provide focus through your organizational structure. The way you choose to organize—around customer segments, geographies, product lines, functions, or anything else—shapes the focus of your organization. In addition to focus, org structure helps define decision rights and accountability. Your org structure will impact your talent management strategy, help or hinder your organizational agility, and influence employee engagement.

Org structure should be thoughtfully designed to serve your strategy and business model, but consider also the implications for innovation that extend beyond the way it might serve to focus our energy and resources. Innovative organizations don't let org structures get in the way of nimbly responding to opportunities. The way I organized my business might not work for others, but I'll share it because it gives me an opportunity to talk about my granddaughter.

Amy is a great student and athlete and wears number 10 on the soccer field. She's now in high school, but I've been attending her games every chance I could since she was very young. The players on Amy's high school team all have assigned positions to play and a skill set to match. Her current team is disciplined, very different from her first team of under-9s in which everyone seemed to have the same position— ball chaser. Watching the little kids play was hilarious. It was like watching a swarm of beetles chasing a rolling ball of dung.

My org structure has elements of both those soccer teams. We have functional pillars, enabling functions such as Finance, IT, HR, Legal, etc., in which employees have assigned roles and responsibilities. They play their positions like the advanced players on Amy's current team. But many of our employees work on project teams that morph and change with the needs of the business and our perception of opportunities. They have bursts of energy. Bursts of focus. They swarm.

However you choose to organize, make sure you build in some ability to swarm in order to seize an opportunity for innovation.

≋ *Clearly define acceptable risk.* You won't learn if you don't take risks. Learning occurs when you risk moving out of your comfort zone and risk making mistakes. So it is with innovation. You won't innovate if you don't take risks.

Just telling employees they're empowered doesn't mean they actually are empowered. And telling employees to take risks doesn't mean they're able to take risks. You need to help them understand the difference between acceptable and unacceptable risk. You need to show them what smart risk looks like and, importantly, what it looks like to take stupid risks.

Give this some serious thought and take the time to develop examples to illustrate what smart and stupid risks look like to you. There's no shortage of innovation gurus who promote the celebration of failure as a way to encourage risk. But this can backfire unless you've clearly defined what you mean by desired and undesired risk. In that case, it's probably OK to celebrate a smart risk that ends in failure.

≋ *Aggressively manage organizational expertise.* Expertise is an important type of capital. You need to conserve it, protect it, and grow it. Create an infrastructure to do this—a defined process, managers who are accountable, and perhaps a structure such as Communities of Practice. Senior leaders need to do whatever it takes to ensure expertise is preserved and disseminated in order to build innovation capability.

It starts with capturing and documenting the tacit expertise of your senior specialists. Don't worry. You don't have to capture the knowledge of all your senior people. Only a small percentage of employees will have acquired a high degree of tacit, mission-critical expertise. In addition to all I've written above about leveraging deep experts and using them to teach and coach others, we implemented several practices that helped us capture and manage expertise and to better innovate:

1. After action reviews. We initially held AARs because clients required them as an embedded process step to conclude projects. The value, though, was apparent, and we adopted the practice internally for nearly all projects. We developed a simple template to guide exploration and documentation of lessons learned over the course of the project. We saved our documentation on a shared drive, and every single person in the organization had access to all AAR documentation for every project.

2. Scenario sessions. These were monthly lunch meetings in which we identified a particular topic or problem and invited interested parties to stump one or two deep experts. We had one or two of our top experts from a key area— usually from material science, tool design, instrumentation, or composite manufacturing— participate on a panel of sorts. We asked the experts to begin by describing a particularly difficult challenge they'd faced and briefly describe their solution. The engineers and technicians who attended posed questions and probed, prodded, and challenged the experts. We all viewed this as kind of a game and had fun with it. But it was serious stuff. Questions explored all aspects of the problem scenario. When experts are pressed to address time, space, and context, the tacit slowly becomes explicit.

I often attended these meeting and joined in the questioning and recognized the experts and participants who had the most insightful questions.

3. Pre-mortems. Innovation requires more than development of a solution. It requires implementation. Before a solution was fully designed and implemented, project teams conducted a pre-mortem in which they tried to envision every conceivable thing that might go wrong with implementation of the solution. They then created plans to mitigate the risk of implementation failure.

Innovation is the way to grow your business profitably. It is incredibly difficult to do well. You need deep experts who, as Yuri did last night, make their craft appear deceptively simple. You need team leaders who are able to get deep experts to play together as a maestro does with an orchestra. And you need senior leaders who can assemble and deploy this talent in an engaging environment.

It's been good for me to reflect this week on all we accomplished in the business. We created an incredible amount of intangible value through our talent, and I'm thinking now that maybe the price I received for the equity stake wasn't at a premium after all.

My cruise is over in a few hours, and I've got just enough time to start drafting a plan for my next venture.

Recommended Reading List

Lombardo, M., & Eichinger, R. (2011). *The Leadership Machine: Architecture to Develop Leaders for Any Future.* Minneapolis, MN: Lominger International: A Korn/Ferry Company.

Becker, B., Huselid, M., & Beatty, R. (2009). *The Differentiated Workforce: Transforming Talent into Strategic Impact.* Boston, MA: Harvard Business Press.

Ulrich, D., & Brockbank, W. (2005). *The HR Value Proposition.* Boston, MA: Harvard Business Press.

Charan, R. (2007). *Leaders at All Levels: Deepening Your Talent Pool to Solve the Succession Crisis.* San Francisco, CA: Jossey-Bass.

Also by Kim Ruyle

FYI for Strategic Effectiveness (2007), with Robert Eichinger and David Ulrich. Minneapolis, MN: Lominger International: A Korn/Ferry Company.

FYI for Performance Management (2007), with Robert Eichinger and Michael Lombardo. Minneapolis, MN: Lominger International: A Korn/Ferry Company.

FYI for Talent Engagement (2009), with Robert Eichinger and Kenneth De Meuse. Minneapolis, MN: Lominger International: A Korn/Ferry Company.

FYI for Insight (2010), with George Hallenbeck, Vicki Swisher, and Evelyn Orr. Minneapolis, MN: Lominger International: A Korn/Ferry Company.

Acknowledgements

I've been privileged to work with and learn from many clients and colleagues from around the world. I'm especially indebted to my friends and colleagues at Korn Ferry and its network of talented associates.

I'm grateful for the input from those who read an early version of my manuscript: Vicki Swisher, Linda Hodge, Beth Summers, Steve Marshall, Julie Scott, Michael Harper, Kate Bett, Michael Friedman, Kye Samuelson, Jim Peters, and Larry Clark. Kimberly Clouse and Bonnie Parks did a wonderful job editing. Thank you to Lesley Kurke for the great formatting and print production advice. Beatriz Marin was the inspiration for the cruise ship setting.

Many years ago, Stanley Easter and Hank Sredl provided me with opportunities that made a difference. In more ways than he knows, Bob Eichinger has stretched my thinking. Covey Ruyle taught me what it means to be talented, and so much more.

Author Biography

Kim Ruyle

Kim Ruyle is president of Inventive Talent Consulting, LLC, where he applies more than thirty years of experience in human resources, organizational development, and general management. His Miami-based firm provides strategic talent management and organizational development consulting for leading global enterprises. A current associate in Korn Ferry's Global Associate Network, he spent nearly six years with Korn Ferry Leadership and Talent Consulting. There, he served as vice president of research and development, leading the development of assessments, human resources tools, and thought leadership. In addition, the author has presented at numerous national and international conferences, has published dozens of articles and book chapters, has served on expert panels and editorial boards, and has coauthored four other books on talent management and leadership development. He currently holds three master's degrees and a PhD.

For more information:

Visit Ruyle's website at www.inventivetalent.com, follow him on Twitter at @inventivetalent, or e-mail him at kim.ruyle@inventivetalent.com.

Inventive Talent Survey™ Innovation Leadership

Innovation drives profitable growth, but leading innovation is one of the most difficult of all leadership challenges. Inventive Talent Consulting has developed a research-based survey of innovation leadership capabilities. The 49-item assessment is administered to selected employees online and provides an Innovation Index score as well as scores in six research-based drivers of innovation. The assessment provides guidance for driving engagement through:

- Enterprise leadership
- Enterprise culture
- Innovation team leadership
- Innovation team dynamics
- Technical talent
- Management of technical career paths

Clients using the Inventive Talent Survey™ of Innovation Leadership can add custom items to the survey and receive:

- Customized feedback report
- Technical report describing research validity and psychometrics
- Innovation literature review summary in .pdf format summarizing the meta-analysis of research that underpins the survey construction

Contact Kim Ruyle at 616-308-3255 by phone or kim.ruyle@inventivetalent.com by email for more information.

Inventive Talent Consulting, LLC
Kim E. Ruyle, President
616-308-3255 | kim.ruyle@inventivetalent.com

KORN FERRY An Independent Lominger Associate
Lominger International; A Korn Ferry Company

Talent innovates. Talent executes. Talent drives organizational performance.

Accelerated Development Program for High Professionals™

Many organizations rely on functional experts to drive innovation and achieve their competitive advantage. Developing leadership capabilities in functional experts is essential but challenging. Fast-track experts, high professionals, generally have different development needs than other high potential talent. They should be developed differently, engaged differently, and deployed into job assignments differently. The Inventive Talent Accelerated Development Program for High Professionals™ is designed to develop the leadership skills required to champion innovation, manage change, and advance to senior strategic roles in your organization.

The Inventive Talent Accelerated Development Program for High Professionals™ is research-based development that is customized to be tightly integrated with your organization's culture and strategy. The program normally meets three times over the course of one year and is facilitated by Kim Ruyle, and selected executives from your organization. In addition to assessments, individualized coaching, and highly interactive team-based activities, the program incorporates action learning assignments that address real world issues faced by your organization.

The Inventive Talent Accelerated Development Program for High Professionals™ is designed to serve emerging high-professional talent, early-career functional experts who demonstrate the following:

- A track record of consistently high performance
- Expertise in and passion for a specialized discipline that is key to the organization's success
- High career motivation and willingness to expend extra time and effort to participate in the program

This program will prepare your high performing experts to effectively lead!

Contact Kim Ruyle at 616-308-3255 by phone or kim.ruyle@inventivetalent.com by email for more information.

Inventive Talent Consulting, LLC
Kim E. Ruyle, President
616-308-3255 | kim.ruyle@inventivetalent.com

KORN FERRY *An Independent Lominger Associate*
Lominger International; A Korn Ferry Company